Socrates Meets Freud

Other Works of Peter Kreeft
from St. Augustine's Press

Philosophy 101 by Socrates
Socrates Meets Descartes
Socrates Meets Hume
Socrates Meets Kant
Socrates Meets Kierkegaard
Socrates Meets Machiavelli
Socrates Meets Marx
Socrates Meets Sartre
The Philosophy of Jesus (also in audio format)
Jesus-Shock (also in audio format)
An Ocean Full of Angels
Summa Philosophica
Socrates' Children: Ancient
Socrates' Children: Medieval
Socrates' Children: Modern
Socrates' Children: Contemporary
Socrates' Children [all four books in one]
Socrates' Students
Platonic Tradition
The Sea Within
I Surf, Therefore I Am
If Einstein Had Been a Surfer
Socratic Logic

Socrates Meets Freud

The Father of Philosophy
Meets the Father of Psychology

Socrates cross-examines the author of
Civilization and Its Discontents.

By Peter Kreeft

St. Augustine's Press
South Bend, Indiana

Copyright © 2014 by Peter Kreeft

All rights reserved. No part of this book may be reproduced, stored in a retrieval system, or transmitted, in any form or by any means, electronic, mechanical, photocopying, recording, or otherwise, without the prior permission of St. Augustine's Press.

Manufactured in the United States of America

1 2 3 4 5 6 19 18 17 16 15 14

Library of Congress Cataloging in Publication Data
Kreeft, Peter.
Socrates meets Freud: the father of philosophy meets the father of psychology / Peter Kreeft.
pages cm
ISBN 978-1-58731-837-5 (pbk.)
1. Freud, Sigmund, 1856–1939. 2. Socrates. 3. Imaginary conversations. I. Title.
BF109.F74K74 2013
150.19'52092 – dc23 2013026617

∞ The paper used in this publication meets the minimum requirements of the American National Standard for Information Sciences Permanence of Paper for Printed Materials, ANSI Z39.481984.

St. Augustine's Press
www.staugustine.net

CONTENTS

Introduction

Probably no single thinker since Jesus has influenced the thoughts and lives of more people living in the Western world today than Sigmund Freud.

Even agnostics like William Barrett, in *Irrational Man*, and atheists like Nietzsche, agree that the single most radical change in the last thousand years of Western civilization has been the decline of religion. And the four most influential critics of religion have certainly been Nietzsche, Marx, Darwin, and Freud. Of the four, Freud is by far the most popular. (Computer-generated name searches reveal that his name appears more than twice as often as any of the other three, in both published books and private letters.)

No name is more associated with, and in fact responsible for, "the sexual revolution" than Freud. And no revolution in history, at least none since the one around a cross and an empty tomb, and perhaps even none since the one around a snake and an apple, has been more life-changing, and has more potential to continue to be more radically life-changing in the future, than the sexual revolution. To see this, just read Huxley's *Brave New World*. (And remember that Huxley was far from being a theist.)

Freud wore three hats. Freud was (1) a practicing psychoanalyst (indeed, the *inventor* of psychoanalysis), (2) a professional theoretical psychologist, and (3) an amateur philosopher. To do justice to Freud we must always distinguish these three dimensions of his thought when evaluating him (though they are obviously connected). For it is quite possible to accept the practical power of psychoanalysis without embracing the theoretical psychological principles behind it (indeed, most psychologists and psychiatrists today describe themselves this way), and equally possible to embrace many of the principles of his psychology without the philosophy, the world-and-life-view, behind it. (Or, for that matter, vice versa.)

This book explores only his philosophy, for that is the point of his intersection with Socrates. If Socrates is right in his deepest convictions about the importance of philosophy, Freud's *philosophy* is the ultimate source, foundation, explanation, and justification for his psychology.

Readers of this book, therefore, should not expect direct evaluations of the famous "Freudian" details of these other two dimensions of Freud's work—not because they are not important, and not because they are unrelated to his philosophy, but because one cannot do everything at once (unless one's proper name is "I AM WHO AM"), and certainly cannot do *justice* to everything at once.

Civilization and its Discontents is Freud's most philosophical work (as well as his last one), for its question, announced in its very first sentence, is nothing but the first and most important question of all great philosophers, the question of the "meaning of life," the ultimate end, greatest good, "summum bonum," highest value, point and purpose of living; the answer to the ultimate "why?"

As with the other books in this series, a "willing

suspension of disbelief" is requested of the reader when it is discovered, at the beginning of the conversation, that Freud has died, has met Socrates in the next world, and is required to undergo a Socratic examination on this book. The locale is something like the Purgatorial porch of Heaven.

Cross-examining other philosophers was the Heaven Socrates most devoutly hoped for; and being cross-examined by him is the Purgatory that most other philosophers most devoutly fear. God is economical: the same setup suffices for one's Heaven and the other's Purgatory. (C. S. Lewis, in another context—the issue of animal immortality and whether it extends to insects—suggests that that same divine efficiency could also combine a Heaven for mosquitoes and a Hell for men.)

1.
The Meeting

FREUD: I exist! I still exist. I thought I just died. But I must be dreaming.

SOCRATES: You did die. And you are not dreaming.

FREUD: That cannot be.

SOCRATES: You can see for yourself that it is. Here you are.

FREUD: But where is "here"?

SOCRATES: It is where you are now. Wherever you are, that's "here."

FREUD: And what is this "I" that is here?

SOCRATES: Ah, now that's the great question, isn't it? "Know thyself," and all that kind of thing. It was your "thing" all your life, as it was mine too, though in exploring our common question we used different methods and came to different conclusions.

FREUD: Why are you impersonating Socrates?

SOCRATES: I am no more impersonating Socrates than you are impersonating Freud.

FREUD: Socrates is dead. You are a fraud.

SOCRATES: I am no more a fraud than you are, Freud. In fact, to assume a bad British accent for the sake of a bad pun, I'm afreud you're a Freud, not a fraud.

FREUD: Am I then in the Hell of Horrible Puns? No, this must be a dream.

SOCRATES: If it is a dream, who is dreaming it?

FREUD: I am, of course.

SOCRATES: But you died.

FREUD: I must have only dreamed that I died.

SOCRATES: But in your psychological works you said that that was the one thing no one could ever dream.

FREUD: Perhaps I was mistaken about that.

SOCRATES: And also about the *I* who made the mistake? I mean about the real existence of the ego? You thought it was only a façade for the id.

FREUD: Perhaps I am just part of an ongoing dream.

SOCRATES: In which case, who is the dreamer? A real *you* can dream of imaginary places, but if the *you* is itself a dream, who is *its* dreamer?

FREUD: The id. The "it." That is the real self, not the conscious ego. Descartes was wrong.

SOCRATES: But this *it* that you say you really are is not an *I*, it is less than an *I*—isn't that what you say?

FREUD: Yes.

SOCRATES: But how can anything *less* than a self dream a self? How can the effect be greater than the cause?

FREUD: You should be arrested for imitating a philosopher.

SOCRATES: It is not a crime to imitate oneself.

FREUD: I know you cannot be Socrates. But, then, I also know that I can't be Freud. Because I no longer exist. I *did* die. I distinctly felt my body fall away from me.

SOCRATES: In that case it logically follows that you are more than your body, you are a self that survives the death of your body. So you were wrong about *that.*

FREUD: It certainly looks like I was wrong about *something.*

SOCRATES: Would you like to find out what some of those somethings were?

FREUD: Of course. Any honest scientist pursues the truth at all costs, even costs to his own self-image. But who are you, really? Or, perhaps I should say *what* are you? Are you my own subconscious? Are you playing the part of a demon from Hell?

SOCRATES: That would indeed be Hell for me, if I were merely your subconscious! No, I am as real as you are, I assure you.

FREUD: And what is that costume you are wearing? You look like I imagine Socrates would look, so I imagine you are a figment of my own imagination.. Appearances are deceiving, as you philosophers well know.

SOCRATES: Sometimes appearances are *not* deceiving.

FREUD: What am I doing here? Where is the bed I was dying in, or lying in? I am utterly confused.

SOCRATES: And I am here to help to un-confuse you, about many things more important than where you are.

FREUD: No, I think it is more likely that you are here to *confuse* me, to make me think that you are the real Socrates, and that this place is something like Heaven.

SOCRATES: Well, there are only a few logical possibilities. Shall we go through them, to try to un-confuse you? That's my thing, after all, as a philosopher.

FREUD: Philosophize away, demon or angel or ghost or subconscious dream or purgatorial spirit or Socrates—or whatever you are.

SOCRATES: You have already very nicely set out the six possibilities..

FREUD: And I'm sure you have logical arguments disproving all five other possibilities, so that the only one left is that you are the real Socrates, as you will try to convince me by pure reason. No, I think not. I am suspicious of your tricks, and of your reliance on reason.

SOCRATES: How could reliance on reason be a trick? Reason is the only way to see *through* tricks and refute them.

FREUD: Whoever or whatever you are, you are at least an authentic fake, a good Socrates imitation. But you are wrong about reason. If there is any one truth I have discovered in a long lifetime devoted to the study of the mind, it is this: that reason is the servant of desire, not the other way round, as *you* thought, "Socrates." What you call reasoning is really rationalizing. There is a far more powerful unconscious and subconscious mind behind your conscious, rational thinking, like a puppeteer behind a puppet.

SOCRATES: Really?

FREUD: Really.

SOCRATES: Let me be your student in this matter, for you have indeed devoted an entire lifetime to the study of the mind, and if there is anyone who is a world-famous authority on the ways it works, it must be you—especially the subconscious and unconscious mind. So let us assume that your primary discovery is true. Now I too have spent a lifetime studying the mind—not the unconscious and irrational mind but the conscious and rational mind. And if there is one thing my lifetime of study has shown me it is that the principles of logic never have any exceptions. If all A is B and all B is C, then all A must always be C. If B necessarily follows A and if A is true, then B must always be true. Now let us assume that your great discovery is true: that all reasoning is really only rationalizing. Let us see what B follows from this assumption A.

FREUD: Why should I play your little logic game with you? You will win. You always do. Because it's *your* game.

SOCRATES: Perhaps it is only my "game," as *you* say, and perhaps, on the other hand, it is *not* only my game but the most basic law of everything that is real and true, as *I* say. But I played your little illogic game with you: I accepted your primary discovery, that all reasoning is only rationalizing. So we are now thinking in terms of *your* world, the world in which your primary discovery is true, not *my* world, in which it is false.

Surely you have no objection to exploring your own world?

FREUD: No.

SOCRATES: Then let us see what this primary discovery of yours actually means. You say that *all* reasoning is rationalizing, is that right?

FREUD: Yes.

SOCRATES: No exceptions?

FREUD: No exceptions.

SOCRATES: Just like my principles of logic in that way: no exceptions.

FREUD: No exceptions.

SOCRATES: So the reasoning by which you arrived at that discovery—that must also have been merely rationalizing, then. And the reasoning by which you affirm it and defend it and argue for it now—that too must be merely rationalizing.

FREUD: Indeed.

SOCRATES: Why, then, should I subject my mind to your private desires? Why should I let myself be a puppet in your puppet theater? Why should I consent to be a character in your dreams or fantasies? And why did you support your principle with so much reasoning and scientific evidence, then, if such reasoning never really proved anything true?

FREUD: You are playing *your* game with me now, Socrates. You are subjecting my psychology to your logic. I could equally well subject your logic to my psychology.

SOCRATES: You could indeed—and the result would be nothing but a personal power struggle, a struggle of wills, my fantasy versus yours, my desires versus yours, my game versus yours. Now that is certainly not the scientific method, is it?

FREUD: No.

SOCRATES: And you are the one who claimed to have applied the scientific method to psychology for the first time, to have turned psychology into a science for the first time. You are that Sigmund Freud, aren't you? Or do I have a case of mistaken identity here?

FREUD: I am that Freud.

SOCRATES: So shouldn't you be playing the scientific game?—if you insist on calling it a "game."

FREUD: I have no objection to being scientific.

SOCRATES: But being scientific means at least being logical, doesn't it?

FREUD: It means much more than that, Socrates. That is what you ancients failed to see. That's why your science was so primitive and unsuccessful.

SOCRATES: Science may indeed mean much more than logic, something more specific; but it certainly can't mean anything less, can it? Can something that is simply illogical be scientific? For instance, if a tiny blue rabbit suddenly appeared on your head, would it be scientific for you to say, "Oh well, tiny blue rabbits just happen," and not look for a scientific explanation of it?

FREUD: Of course not.

SOCRATES: So you agree that even if science is more than logic, it is not less?

FREUD: Yes, I suppose I must agree with that.

SOCRATES: So let us look at what the two of us mean by logic. I think it is pretty much the same thing. In fact, I think everyone in the world means essentially the same thing by it. Let me see if I am right in thinking that. Suppose I told you that I believed that all A is B and all B is C, but I did not believe that all A is C simply because I did not *want* to believe that. You would not call that scientific, would you? And you would say it is unscientific because it is illogical, wouldn't you?

FREUD: Give me a concrete example.

SOCRATES: Gladly. Suppose I believed that all humans must die and that I was a human, but I did not believe that I would ever die, because I did not *want* to believe that. Would you call my state of mind either scientific or logical?

FREUD: Of course not.

SOCRATES: How would you explain it?

FREUD: I would call it fantasizing, or wishful thinking. You are rationalizing your desires. None of us desires to die, but to live.

SOCRATES: I would agree with that. So you *are* playing my "game" of science and logic with me, as you put it.

FREUD: I have no objection to logic.

SOCRATES: Good. So let us look at the logical consequence of your principle that all reasoning is only rationalizing. Since that principle is a matter of reasoning, and was reached by reasoning, and is defended by reasoning, it logically follows that it too is nothing but rationalizing.

FREUD: I accept that logical conclusion.

SOCRATES: Thank you. When I drew that logical conclusion a little while ago, you objected that I was trying to get you to play "my game." Now it seems that "my" game is your game too, and that you have no objection to playing it with me. And I have no objection in playing "your game" of psychology with you. So it seems that both our "games," as you put it, are at least sharable in principle, and in fact are here and now being shared by both of us. Am I right about that, or am I being too optimistic?

FREUD: You are right about that, though I do *not* believe you are right about there being a single objective and universal and timeless truth behind your logic. I will obey the rules of logic not because I claim to know that it mirrors things-in-themselves or objective reality, as you believe, but because we all agree to play by its rules. But even though our reasons for accepting the rules of logic are different, we can agree to play by them wherever we are, even here—wherever "here" is.

SOCRATES: That is sufficient for now. Then let us turn to your book, which is to be the subject of our discussion.

2.
The Question

FREUD: As soon as you mentioned it, the book appeared in my hand! This *must* be a dream. Things like that do not happen in the real world.

SOCRATES: Not in that other world, the world you once lived in. But you live in that world no longer, Sigmund.

FREUD: And yet I live.

SOCRATES: Yes. Does it not follow, then, that this is another world?

FREUD: Yes, but it does not follow that that other world is a real one. It may be only the world of my dreams and fantasies, or of someone else's.

SOCRATES: I will not try to prove you wrong there, for that would be a diversion and distraction from our purpose, which is to explore your book. Let's just suspend judgment about that question and proceed *as if* we were both equally real persons in a commonly real world. Can you do that?

FREUD: I can. But why should I?

SOCRATES: Because it would be profitable for you.

FREUD: Why?

SOCRATES: Because the subject of our discussion is to be your book, your most philosophical book, your last complete book, and your most important one.

FREUD: A book is only a product of the mind behind it. So what you really want to investigate is my mind—in fact me, and not just my book. Isn't that right, Socrates?

SOCRATES: Actually, it is *both*, and each is a means to the other: understanding your book will help both of us to understand yourself better, and understanding yourself will help both of us to understand your book better.

FREUD: That is a sound psychological principle. In fact, it is a good way of doing what you yourself claimed to do, Socrates—or Socrates-imitator, whoever you are—when you said that you took the oracle's first commandment, "know thyself," as your life's motto.

SOCRATES: In a sense the two of us were doing two different aspects of that very same thing with our lives—the thing I called philosophy and the thing you called psychology.

FREUD: Yes.

SOCRATES: But these two things differed in many important ways.

FREUD: What ways? How do you see their differences?

SOCRATES: Well, for one thing, my philosophy sought a knowledge that was more universal, that *included* psychology as well as many other things.

FREUD: Yes. And I was suspicious of that claim to universal knowledge.

SOCRATES: And there was a second difference: you explored the subjective and I explored the objective.

FREUD: Yet we overlapped here, in the "self," and the "know thyself."

SOCRATES: That is true. And there was a third difference, in our *methods:* philosophy, or at least my brand of it, was more a matter of deductive logical reasoning, while psychology, or at least your brand of it, was more a matter of induction and scientific method: testing hypotheses by empirical data.

FREUD: Indeed. That is a great difference. That is why there was more progress in psychology than in philosophy.

SOCRATES: I think that is not as great a difference as you think. I too tested hypotheses by data, but my data were not merely empirical.

FREUD: That's why your theories were not objectively verifiable or falsifiable, as mine were.

SOCRATES: I would dispute both parts of that opinion.

I think you would have to admit that my theories were objectively verifiable just as yours were, if only you broadened your notion of what is "objective" to include anything beyond the empirical—that is, if only you did not make a very questionable philosophical assumption called materialism.

And not only was my work as verifiable as yours, but yours was at least as unverifiable as mine. Many of your theories will be criticized by many scientists as unscientific precisely because they were not conclusively falsifiable in principle. For instance, *any* psychological data that you discovered by experience, in therapy or anywhere else, would be classified according to your a priori categories of id, ego and superego, so that these categories could not in principle be falsifiable, and therefore could not in principle be conclusively verifiable either.

FREUD: That is a severe challenge to my claim to be scientific. It demands a thorough and careful investigation.

SOCRATES: It does. But not now. We are here to discuss your book, which is about something much more practical than the correct theory of scientific method. It is about what people usually call "the meaning of life," or values. May I begin questioning you about it now?

FREUD: You may. Where will you begin?

SOCRATES: Where *you* begin, of course. Here is your first sentence, which asks the great question, the question all the great philosophers ask:

It is impossible to escape the impression that people commonly use false standards of measurement—that they seek power, success and wealth for themselves and admire them in others, and that they underestimate what is of true value in life.

Am I correct in assuming that this is the question of the book, the question of "what is of true value in life"?

FREUD: That is correct.

SOCRATES: And that this involves what you call "measurement," or judgment—value judgment?

FREUD: Yes.

SOCRATES: And you criticize those who "**seek power, success and wealth as their values.**"

FREUD: Yes.

SOCRATES: Thus you assume that such value judgments can be false as well as true, as judgments of empirical facts can be false or true.

FREUD: Yes. But the methods used are very different.

SOCRATES: Evidently. We cannot use merely empirical methods, such as statistics or cameras, for judging values.

FREUD: That is true. But I would not totally separate empirical facts from values. Facts are certainly relevant to values, and values to facts.

SOCRATES: I agree.

FREUD: In fact, everything is relevant to everything.

SOCRATES: I agree with that too. And since values are *qualities* while mathematics deals only with *quantities*, we cannot use merely mathematical standards for judging values either, isn't that right? For instance, we cannot say that wealth and power are greater values than knowledge and understanding simply because a greater number of people prefer them, can we? Or that a man with two million dollars is twice as great a *man* as someone with only with one million?

FREUD: No, of course not.

SOCRATES: Then you are, in this book, at least, asking a profoundly *philosophical* question.

FREUD: Let it be so, then. But since everything is relevant to everything, my psychology is relevant to this philosophical question, and empirical science is relevant to my psychology, and therefore even to this philosophical question.

SOCRATES: I do not deny your logic there.

But I have another question for you now. Why, after raising this great question in your very first sentence, did you not directly answer it, or try to answer it, or even mention it, but instead you spent the rest of chapter 1 investigating an apparently different question, namely the psychological origin of religion?

FREUD: That is an easy question to answer. Do you remember agreeing, just a moment ago, with my principle that everything is relevant to everything?

SOCRATES: I do.

FREUD: Then these two questions are relevant to each other.

SOCRATES: I do not doubt that, but I wonder just *how* they are connected in your mind.

FREUD: Isn't it obvious? How do the vast majority of people in all times, places and cultures, answer this great question? By their religion, of course. Isn't that an observable fact?

SOCRATES: It is.

FREUD: So if we can understand the true origin of religious beliefs, we can evaluate this most popular of all answers first, before proceeding to explore more scientific answers.

SOCRATES: I see. So that is why you do a psychology of religion first?

FREUD: Yes.

3.
The Critique of Religion

SOCRATES: Do you see the assumption that you are making here?

FREUD: Of course. I assume that rival answers cannot both be true; that if religion's answer to this question is not true, then we must seek some nonreligious answers.

SOCRATES: That assumption is just the law of noncontradiction. That is not a questionable assumption. I was thinking of an assumption that is not only questionable but questioned. In fact it is denied by not just a few but most people. And you do not even attempt to prove this questionable assumption.

FREUD: What assumption is that?

SOCRATES: You don't see it?

FREUD: No.

SOCRATES: It is very simple and very obvious. I am surprised that you as a psychologist do not see it. Let me try to help you find it yourself. Suppose I am 50 years old and I tell you that I believe that I will live at least until I am 60. Do you ask me why I would believe that?

FREUD: No.

SOCRATES: Why not?

FREUD: Because nearly everyone who reaches 50 reaches 60.

SOCRATES: So it is a very reasonable belief.

FREUD: Yes.

SOCRATES: Now suppose I tell you that I believe I will live until I am 90. What do you say?

FREUD: I ask you why you believe that.

SOCRATES: Why?

FREUD: Because at least half the 50-year-olds do not reach 90.

SOCRATES: So you ask me for evidence, for reasons, such as my state of health and how old my parents lived to be.

FREUD: Yes.

SOCRATES: So that might be a reasonable belief, or not, depending on the evidence.

FREUD: Yes.

SOCRATES: Therefore we need to examine the evidence.

FREUD: Exactly.

SOCRATES: Now suppose I tell you that I will live until 150 years old. What do you say?

FREUD: I say that is ridiculous.

SOCRATES: Do you ask me for my health records?

FREUD: No.

SOCRATES: Why not?

FREUD: Because the idea is so ridiculous that it does not deserve a logical refutation.

SOCRATES: Exactly. So what would you say to someone who believes he will live until 150?

FREUD: I would examine his irrational desires and fears, especially his fear of death. I would ask him about traumatic deaths in his family, for instance.

SOCRATES: You would psychoanalyze him.

FREUD: Yes.

SOCRATES: You would not reason with him on the conscious level of evidence and argument, but you would probe his unconscious or subconscious mind.

FREUD: Exactly.

SOCRATES: And now in the beginning of your book you are psychoanalyzing religion, looking for the unconscious origin of religious beliefs, rather than arguing for or against these beliefs by means of logic and evidence and argument. You do not mention the problem of evil, for instance, which is the most popular and the most logical argument for atheism. Nor do you mention the argument from order and design in nature, which is a popular argument for theism. Instead, you compare two different theories about the unconscious *origin* of religious beliefs: your friend's theory, which he calls "the oceanic feeling," and your own theory, which is about childhood fears.

FREUD: Yes.

SOCRATES: Do you still not see the assumption you are making?

FREUD: I am assuming that religion is not true, of course.

SOCRATES: Indeed you are. But is that an "of course"?

FREUD: Are you challenging me to prove my atheism now?

SOCRATES: No. I am asking you why you assume it rather than trying to prove it. And I am pointing out that you are assuming not only that atheism is true but also that religion is not worth arguing about, that it is *not* like the idea that I will live until 60, which most reasonable people would believe, or like the idea that I will live until 90, which many reasonable people would believe, but like the idea that I will live until 150, which nearly all reasonable people would find not only untrue but ridiculous. But religion, whether true or false, is not an idea that nearly all people find ridiculous. So either you are wrong or nearly all people are not reasonable people.

FREUD: That depends on which group of people you are listening to, Socrates. You speak of the masses. The proportion of believers and unbelievers is quite the opposite among the educated, and among scientists, and among moderns, and among those who have experienced what historians call the Enlightenment.

SOCRATES: In other words, among those whose level of intelligence fits them to be your readers.

FREUD: Exactly.

SOCRATES: I would like to ask you three questions about a certain word, Sigmund.

FREUD: Ask away, Socrates.

SOCRATES: The word is "snobbery." First, would you agree that it is a mistake? And second, would you agree that an example of it would be the belief that only a tiny minority of people, namely yourself and the people who are like you, and believe the same things that you believe, are truly reasonable or wise enough to live in the real world and not in dreams and illusions, and that the vast majority of all other humans who have ever lived or who now live, in all times and places and cultures, are very unwise and live in great illusion—would that not be an example of snobbery? And third, would you agree that if we were to use the principles of logic and use these first two beliefs as premises—that snobbery is a mistake and that your belief is an example of snobbery—that the logical conclusion would be that your assumption here is a mistake?

FREUD: That is an *ad hominem* argument, Socrates—as you should know if you are an expert in logic.

SOCRATES: And what is an *ad hominem* argument?

FREUD: It is an attack on the arguer instead of the argument.

SOCRATES: Quite right. But I showed that your *idea* was snobbery, Sigmund. I attacked your argument, not you.

FREUD: Who but a snob would have snobbish ideas? If it looks like a duck and it walks like a duck and it sounds like a duck, it's a duck. If you have the beliefs of a snob, you are a snob.

SOCRATES: Well, then, since you clearly have the beliefs of a snob—you see what follows. But it is neither you nor even your beliefs that I am quarreling with, but your procedure. You do not *argue*. You simply *assume* that religious beliefs—the beliefs of the vast majority—are not only false but so absurd that the only reasonable approach to them is not argument but psychoanalysis. You *assume,* at the very beginning, that religion is not only false but absurd, so absurd that it deserves no logical refutation, but only psychoanalysis; that it is like the belief that I will live to 150.

FREUD: I have already given my reasons and evidence against religion in two other books, *Moses and Monotheism* and *The Future of an Illusion.*

SOCRATES: But you did the very same thing there as you did here, though with far greater and cleverer detail: you simply *assumed* without question that religion was untrue. And then you gave a very clever and elaborate explanation—a quite reasonable and persuasive one, by the way—of the origin of this illusion. It is perhaps the very best psychological explanation of the origin of religion ever given, *assuming* that religion is false. So atheists are rightly grateful for your explanation. But you only explained a possible *origin* of the belief. You did not prove the belief *false.*

FREUD: But it was not my purpose in this book to prove atheism, any more than it was the purpose of the writings of the saints to prove theism. Their purpose was simply to explore the psychological consequences of their belief. Mine was simply to explore the psychological origin of it.

SOCRATES: But in your book you do not explore either the logical reasons for or the psychological origins of your belief, your atheism and your materialism and your "pleasure principle"— because you *assume* that they are reasonable, like the belief that I shall live to my 60s.

All you do to your beliefs in your books is what the saints do to their beliefs in their books: you trace their consequences.

FREUD: This is true. So what?

SOCRATES: How can that be fair? You explore only the origins, not the consequences, of their belief, and you explore only the consequences, not the origins, of yours. Why? I can think of only one answer to that question: you assume that atheism is so obviously true and theism so obviously false that atheism needs to be treated logically and theism psychoanalyzed.

FREUD: Well, of course.

SOCRATES: But it is not an "of course." It is a momentous question, and a controversial one.

FREUD: But there are abundant reasons for atheism and against theism: psychological reasons, historical reasons, logical reasons, and scientific reasons. But that was not the purpose of my book. One cannot do everything in any one book. Could we please explore what I did say in this book rather than arguing about what you think I should have said?

SOCRATES: Yes, of course. But I was not arguing that you "should have said" something else. I was not telling you what to say, just exploring the logic of what you said.

FREUD: Let's do that, then, instead of talking about it.

SOCRATES: I think it is quite easy to summarize. You compare two theories of the origin of religion: your own and your friend's. (Romain Rolland was his name, I believe.) Your friend thought the origin of religion was the blissful "oceanic feeling," the feeling that all of reality is a single ocean, with no shore, so that "**we cannot fall out of this world**" because we are all one divine and immortal ocean of being. This sounds like a kind of Eastern pantheistic mysticism, which denies the reality of the separate individual ego, the "I."

FREUD: I do not wholly reject what my friend said. For one thing, I do not deny that this feeling exists, though I have never experienced it, nor that it may be the origin of some religion. I also agree with those mystics about one thing: that the ego is not the separate reality it appears to be. I wrote:

This ego appears to us as something autonomous and unitary, marked off distinctly from everything else. That such an appearance is deceptive, and that on the contrary the ego is continued inwards, without any sharp delimitation, into an unconscious mental entity which we designate as the id and for which it serves as a kind of façade—this was a discovery first made by psycho-analytic research.

I then offered the analogy of an ancient city—Rome or Troy—that has many layers of history under its present surface. They appear only to archeological digging. Psychoanalysis is like that digging, and it finds many other, deeper layers underneath the surface or façade of the ego.

I realize that this is a startling idea to the Western mind. Ever since Descartes, we in the West have tended to think that our first and most unassailable certainty is the conscious, rational self that thinks: "I think, therefore I am." But I say that this rational ego is much less than it seems.

SOCRATES: So that is how you agree with Eastern religions: in what they deny, not in what they affirm.

FREUD: Yes. I do not believe in Atman or Brahman or the Buddha-mind or the Tao. These religions dissolve the ego into something greater. I dissolve it into something less: into the impersonal id, the "it."

SOCRATES: And what about Western religions?

FREUD: Western religions are the opposite of Eastern on this point: they say that the individual human self or ego is much *more* than it seems: it is a "child of God," something not only substantial and intrinsically precious but immortal.

SOCRATES: So when you sail away from the East's religions you do not sail West, and when you sail away from the West you do not sail East.

FREUD: No, I agree with Eastern religions in their denial of the reality of the individual ego, but not in their affirmation of the cosmic super-ego.

SOCRATES: So since you do not accept your friend's theory that the mystical "oceanic feeling" is the origin of religion, can you summarize very simply your alternative answer to that question?

FREUD: It is essentially that we created God in our own image rather than vice versa. More specifically, God the Father is a substitute for the inadequate or missing earthly father. I wrote that **The derivation of religious needs from the infant's helplessness and the longing for the father aroused by it seems to me incontrovertible . . . I cannot think of any need in childhood as strong as the need for a father's protection.**

SOCRATES: Not even the need for the mother's milk and the mother's touch?

FREUD: Perhaps both needs are at work.

SOCRATES: If so, would that explain why Eastern religions posit an immanent mother-God while Western religions posit a transcendent father-God?

FREUD: Perhaps. It is a hypothesis worth investigating some other time.

SOCRATES: But the thing you call "incontrovertible" is your reduction of religion to infantile needs.

FREUD: Yes.

SOCRATES: So that is your assumption, then?

FREUD: No, not in a dogmatic way. It is not an alternative *religion* for me, as you implied. It is testable by reason.

SOCRATES: Religious believers claim that the religious hypothesis is testable by reason too. For many centuries many of them have been engaging in what they call apologetics, giving reasons for their faith.

FREUD: But not by the scientific method. You know the scientific method, do you not?

SOCRATES: Know it? I invented much of it, I think.

FREUD: Then you know that there are at least five steps to this method. First, we begin with a question. Second, we proceed to gather relevant data. Third, we form a hypothesis to explain the data. Fourth, we test the hypothesis by predicting what data we would observe if the hypothesis were true, and then observing how well the data confirm the hypothesis. Finally, if there is enough confirmation by the data, we raise the hypothesis to the status of a theory, and then, if conclusively confirmed, a fact.

SOCRATES: I understand.

FREUD: Well, the first point, the question, is: What is the origin of religion?

SOCRATES: That's clear.

FREUD: Second, the data consist in what religion is, what it claims, what it does for man. This is what I explore in my book *The Future of an Illusion,* in which I summarize the data in two major categories.

The first is what makes religion attractive to human *minds.* Our minds are weak and puzzled when faced with the mysteries of life and death and man's place in the cosmos. Religion claims to answer the questions we find the most important and at the same time the most difficult: questions about ultimate purposes and destinies, and why we exist.

The second category is what makes religion attractive to *feelings,* especially the feeling of fear, which, given our ignorance and weakness, is one of the strongest of all emotions, if not the very strongest. Religion assures us that there is a God who is not only wise but also benevolent and who is totally in charge of all things.

These two deep human desires correspond exactly to the two things every religion offers. Thus I summarize my earlier book's conclusions under the headings of "doctrines and promises," in these words:

In my *Future of an Illusion,* I was concerned . . . with what the common man understands by his religion—with the system of doctrines and promises which on the one hand explains to him the riddles of this world with enviable completeness, and, on the other, assures him that a careful Providence will watch over

his life and will compensate him in a future existence for any frustrations he suffers here.

And then I explain how both of these two abstract selling points are joined in the single concrete figure of the Father-God: **The common man cannot imagine this Providence otherwise than in the figure of an enormously exalted father. Only such a being can understand the needs of the children of men and be softened by their prayers and placated by the signs of their remorse.**

So the data is simply what religion looks like, what it claims. And that is essentially these two things, divine omniscience and divine Providence, united in the cosmic father-figure.

SOCRATES: I see. That is the second step of the scientific method. What is the third?

FREUD: I form a hypothesis that explains the data. It is the hypothesis that God is unconsciously invented by man's mind to fit its needs, like a glove being fitted to a hand. The match is so close that it is a blatantly obvious example of wishful thinking. As Voltaire said, "If God did not exist, it would be necessary to invent Him."

And this match between the hypothesis and the data is really step four, the confirmation of the hypothesis. For if the hypothesis is true, we would find exactly the data we do find. If we did invent God, it would have been exactly the kind of God we find in religion.

SOCRATES: You realize, of course, that as an argument that is an example of the fallacy of "affirming the consequent": *if* we invented God, we would find this kind of God; and we do find this kind of God, therefore we invented God. That is like saying that *if* a very clever demon were hypnotizing us to see and feel an unreal world that looked like earth, then we would see and feel air and water and rocks and all the rest; and we do see and feel all this, therefore there is a very clever demon hypnotizing us.

FREUD: I do not claim that it is a proof. It is merely a match: the very match the scientific method demands.

SOCRATES: Go on, then—though I do not see how it is any different from the hypothesis of the clever demon.

FREUD: Next, we judge *how well* the hypothesis has been confirmed. And the confirmation is perfect, because the match is perfect. Finger by finger, the religious glove fits the human hand. Is it not obvious that the hand fashioned the glove to fit itself? It is far too perfect a fit to be a coincidence. It raises the hypothesis to the status of a convincing theory, if not a fact.

SOCRATES: That still sounds like the fallacious argument that if God did not exist, then we would find exactly the kind of religion we do find, one in which people believe there is a God which satisfies their two deepest needs, which could not be satisfied without such a God. And we do find exactly that kind of religion. Therefore there is no God.

FREUD: I do not claim it is a logical demonstration. But surely the data make the hypothesis extremely probable, if not quite proving it with logical certainty. The fit between the hand and the glove—surely it is not a mere coincidence.

SOCRATES: No, I do not think it is.

FREUD: Then why are you skeptical about my conclusion?

SOCRATES: I think I can show you why. You admit the law of non-contradiction, do you not?

FREUD: Of course.

SOCRATES: So there are only two possibilities. Either there is a God or there is not.

FREUD: Yes.

SOCRATES: And the data are nicely explained by *one* of these two hypotheses: your atheism.

FREUD: Precisely.

SOCRATES: But if the data are equally well explained by *both* of these two hypotheses, how can you say that one of them is much more probable than the other? But you say that atheism is not just more probable but certain, or nearly certain.

FREUD: You mean perhaps the fit is explained by God designing us in His image instead of our designing Him in ours?

SOCRATES: Something like that, yes.

FREUD: But how could that be? How could a glove design a hand?

SOCRATES: I think we are taking our analogy too literally. The logical point is that if there were a God, and He designed us to need Him and want Him and feel our way to Him through our needs and wants, then would we not find exactly the data that we do find?

FREUD: Well, theoretically, I suppose . . .

SOCRATES: So the data would follow equally from both hypotheses, and be equally explained by both hypotheses.

FREUD: Not equally, no.

SOCRATES: Why not?

FREUD: It would take a long time to answer that question, Socrates. It is not an easy question to answer.

SOCRATES: Then, if "it is not an easy question to answer," how can you say, when you describe this religious hypothesis that **The whole thing is so patently infantile, so foreign to reality, that to anyone with a friendly attitude to humanity it is painful to think that the great majority of mortals will never be able to rise above this view of life.**

If I were a poker player I would call this bluffing. If I were a logician I would call it begging the question, assuming what you claim to prove. If I were a rhetorician I would call it jargon or name-calling. And if I were a psychologist I would call it snobbery, when you call the other hypothesis "***patently*** **infantile.**"

FREUD: Are you a missionary spy, Socrates?

SOCRATES: A what?

FREUD: Why are you arguing for religion? I thought the historical Socrates was an agnostic. You are a fake; you are a bad imitation of the real thing.

SOCRATES: I am not arguing for theism but only for logic. And you are not arguing for your atheism, but assuming it.

FREUD: We all have assumptions, Socrates. No one can prove *everything.*

SOCRATES: True. My point is only that we do not need

to make any *assumptions* about religion, either pro or con, to explore the question of "what is of true value in life." All we need to assume is the rules of logic and common human experience. And I would like to continue that exploration now, in a truly agnostic way, without assumptions, if you are willing.

FREUD: I am willing. Proceed.

4.
Changing the Question from the Objective to the Subjective.

SOCRATES: You state the fundamental problem of the book, which is also the fundamental problem of human life, a second time at the beginning of chapter II, but this time you state it negatively rather than positively. In chapter I, you asked "what is of true value in life?" And the answer is, of course, happiness, just as Aristotle said. (I think, by the way, that you mean something very different by "happiness" than he did, as we shall see soon.) But here, in chapter II, you ask how we can avoid *un*happiness.

FREUD: It is logically the same question, since a double negative equals a positive.

SOCRATES: And your answer here, in a single word, is "civilization," by which you mean all the artifices, all the "auxiliary constructions," as you put it, that we devise as means to that end, which is the maximization of happiness or the minimization of unhappiness. Is that a fair summary?

FREUD: Yes. And the fundamental paradox of my book is indicated in its title: the very civilization that we devise to give us contentment, or happiness, makes us *dis*content, or unhappy.

SOCRATES: So that is the fundamental puzzle of the book, then?

FREUD: Yes. And it is not only a *theoretical* puzzle but also a *practical* problem. In chapter II I state the problem this way: **Life, as we find it, is too hard for us; it brings us too many pains, disappointments and impossible tasks. In order to bear it we cannot dispense with palliative measures. "We cannot do without auxiliary constructions," as Theodor Fontane tells us.**

SOCRATES: And these "auxiliary constructions" constitute "civilization?"

FREUD: Yes.

SOCRATES: It is a very broad term, then, the way you use it. It includes everything from technology to the rules of family dynamics.

FREUD: That is why the very next thing I do is to break it into more specific parts, which I classify from a psychological point of view. I say **There are perhaps three such measures: powerful deflections, which cause us to make light of our misery; substitutive satisfactions, which diminish it; and intoxicating substances, which make us insensitive to it.**

SOCRATES: Could you explain that by some examples?

FREUD: Easily. If we are in pain, we seek three things: diversions, pleasures, and anesthetics. Imagine a woman in the pains of childbirth. She might first of all count her breathing, like a practitioner of yoga. Why? It is a mental diversion from the physical pain. Or she might seek the presence and the embrace of her husband to be assured of his love, or she might anticipate the joys of raising her child. Those do not divert or diminish the pain, but they add pleasures to stack against the pain. Or, most obviously, she might ask for a drug to anaesthetize her pain somatically. The other two measures were psychical; this one is somatic, and of course, it is the most direct and the most effective measure.

SOCRATES: Have you ever questioned that assumption?

FREUD: It is not an assumption, it is an observation.

SOCRATES: I think it *is* an assumption, and one which many people would not make. It is your materialism speaking, and most people are not materialists.

FREUD: But surely anesthetics are the single most important invention in recorded history—at least after the control of fire, animals, and agriculture. Most people, if they had to choose to give up any one invention in history, would not give up anesthetics. They would sacrifice any other invention before that one. Imagine living in a world without anesthetics. Imagine expecting at least ten times the amount and intensity of pain in your life that you now expect.

SOCRATES: That is probably true. Most people would make that choice.

FREUD: But *you* would not agree with that choice, Socrates, would you? For you always maintained that the spiritual soul was not only a real entity but the most important thing, far more important than the body.

SOCRATES: We are here to question your philosophy, not mine.

FREUD: All right, what do you question about mine now?

SOCRATES: I wonder why you now suddenly become a populist with regard to human opinion.

FREUD: Instead of the snob you called me earlier?

SOCRATES: Yes—though I did not actually call you a snob; I did not put that shoe on your foot but merely called your attention to the fit.

FREUD: Like Cinderella. Thank you for the left-handed compliment.

SOCRATES: Oh—did you interpret it as a compliment?

FREUD: Are you here to psychoanalyze me or to analyze my book?

SOCRATES: Touché, Sigmund. Your book. Back to the text.

The next thing we find in your text is that you say you have to change the question from something objective to something subjective, because the objective question simply cannot be answered. You say:

The question of the purpose of human life has been raised countless times; it has never yet received a satisfactory answer (I wonder how you know that!) **and perhaps does not admit of one.** (Sometimes "perhaps" is the most precious word we can say!) **Some of those who have asked it have added that if it should turn out that life has *no* purpose, it would lose all value for them. But this threat alters nothing. It looks, on the contrary, as though one had a right to dismiss the question, for it seems to derive from the human presumptuousness,**

many other manifestations of which are already familiar to us.

I have a few questions to ask you about this passage.

FREUD: Why am I not surprised by that?

SOCRATES: First, nearly every important philosopher in history has given an answer to this great question. How do you know that not one of these many answers is satisfactory? Have you fairly examined and explored every one of them?

FREUD: Of course not.

SOCRATES: Then how do you know that none of these answers can possibly be correct?

FREUD: Because they all presuppose the same false premise: that human reason can know the universal and objective truth about the meaning of life. The question is a wild goose chase. No one has ever caught that goose, or ever will. It does not exist. There *is* no one correct answer to that question.

SOCRATES: How do you know that?

FREUD: Very simply. If there *were* one correct answer to that question, as there is one correct answer to empirical or scientific questions, we would have found it and agreed about it. But we have never done that. As the master of logic, you see what follows.

SOCRATES: I wonder how you can prove either of *those* two premises.

As for the second one, how do you know we have never done it? You already admitted that you have not explored and refuted every single answer ever given to that question.

And as for your first premise, how do you know that if there were one correct answer to that question, we would have found it and agreed about it? Surely there are many questions with only one correct answer but the correct answer is not yet known or, if known by a few, is not agreed to by others. For instance, the question Does God exist?

FREUD: But science provides at least the *way* to come to know the truth, and the only way that produces agreement. Science settles questions. Philosophy doesn't. And since science can't settle the question of the meaning of life, it will never be settled.

SOCRATES: I see. You assume, then, that science provides not only *a* way to know the truth but *the* way, the only way.

FREUD: The only way to be *certain*, at least, yes. It is the only way we have ever found.

SOCRATES: I must once again question *that* assumption: that science provides the *only* way to know the truth with certainty.

FREUD: What other way could there be? Do you have one in mind, Socrates?

SOCRATES: I don't claim to know what other ways there might be, but that does not mean they do not exist—unless existence is limited to what I know. You surely do not want to assume *that,* do you? That would be the equivalent of saying I was God.

FREUD: Of course not. Don't be silly, Socrates.

SOCRATES: But you do seem to be assuming that about yourself, though not about me.

FREUD: What a ridiculous thing to charge an atheist with! Why?

SOCRATES: Because you are assuming that other ways do not exist simply because you do not know of them.

FREUD: No, I do not assume that. I am open-minded. If such a way appeared, I would not refuse it in principle. It's just that none has ever appeared that withstands scrutiny. I have indeed explored and examined many candidates—religion and philosophy and tradition and so-called common sense. And it seems to me that all of them are easily refutable.

SOCRATES: By being explainable as projections of unconscious desire, wish-fulfillment? The domination of the "pleasure principle"?

FREUD: Something like that, yes.

SOCRATES: But even though they may be explainable as illusions, they are not all logically impossible, logically inconsistent, logically self-contradictory, are they?

FREUD: No. Illusions are often quite consistent.

SOCRATES: But *your* position is not even logically consistent. What you say contradicts itself, while what I say does not.

FREUD: Why?

SOCRATES: Because to say what I say—that the scientific method is *not* the only way to certain truth—is not self-contradictory, but to say what you say—that it is—*is* self-contradictory.

FREUD: How is it self-contradictory?

SOCRATES: Because if that principle were true, then we could never know that it was true, since the principle itself cannot be proved by the scientific method.

FREUD: Why not?

SOCRATES: Because the scientific method demands empirical proof; but there is no empirical proof of a non-empirical thing, and your principle about the scientific method being the only way to certain truth is not an empirical thing. It is a universal principle, not an observable particular.

FREUD: That is a problem for a logician to work out. It is too abstract for me. Science works. That is all I care about.

SOCRATES: Oh. I thought you cared about truth.

FREUD: Sarcasm is not logic, Socrates. Do you have any other questions?

SOCRATES: Yes. I have a second question about this passage in your book. Do you then believe that life in fact has no purpose?

FREUD: Yes, no objective and universal purpose, although each one of us may construct a subjective and individual purpose. That is how I change the question, so that the investigation can still continue in this more modest way. I reduce the question from a presumptuous one to a non-presumptuous one. This comes out in my very next paragraph, where I say: **We will therefore turn to the less ambitious question of what men themselves show by their behavior to be the purpose and intention of their lives.**

SOCRATES: That is clear. But I have a third question about what you say about life's purpose. You say that for many people, "if it should turn out that life has *no* purpose, it would lose all value for them." Whence do you say comes this universal *demand* for meaning?

FREUD: It is not universal, it is only common. The many, who are the weak, cannot live without it. That is why they turn to religion.

SOCRATES: Some of the strong cannot live without it either. Would you call such thinkers as Plato, Aristotle, Augustine, and Aquinas "weak"?

FREUD: They did not know psychology.

SOCRATES: What do you say about psychologists like Carl Jung and Viktor Frankl, who claim that a comprehensive vision of life is the single most demanding need in human nature?

FREUD: I never heard of those psychologists.

SOCRATES: And therefore . . .

FREUD: More innuendo, Socrates. Don't you know what an innuendo is?

SOCRATES: What?

FREUD: An Italian suppository.

SOCRATES: Good for you, Sigmund: a real sense of humor! Seriously, you've heard of Nietzsche, haven't you?

FREUD: Of course.

SOCRATES: Do you say he is a small, weak mind?

FREUD: No, a great one. A passionate and eloquent atheist.

SOCRATES: What do you think he meant by saying that "a man can endure almost any *how* if only he has a *why*" ?

FREUD: What do *you* think he meant?

SOCRATES: Obviously, that we can endure great suffering if only we believe it has a true and real and objective meaning—labor pains are an obvious example—but we resent even minor inconveniences if we believe they are meaningless, that they serve no necessary purpose.

FREUD: So what is your point?

SOCRATES: I ask you: Where does this demand for meaning come from, if not from human nature itself?

FREUD: Of course it comes from human nature. It comes from human presumptuousness.

SOCRATES: Are you, then, one of the few who lack this presumptuousness?

FREUD: As you say, Socrates, if the shoe fits, wear it.

SOCRATES: And what are some of the "**many other manifestations**" of this presumptuousness that you speak of in this passage?

FREUD: Religion, of course, is the main example. In fact, the very next thing I say is that **Only religion can answer the question of the purpose of life . . .**

SOCRATES: A surprising thing for an atheist to say!

FREUD: Not a *rational* atheist. For I explain the logical connection between these two ideas—that religion is true and that life has a real, objective purpose—in the very next sentence:

One can hardly be wrong in concluding that the idea of life having a purpose stands and falls with the religious system.

SOCRATES: I understand your reasoning, I think. If life is designed by a God, then it is meaningful, as a book is meaningful because it reflects the author's intelligence and design. But if life is not designed by a God, then it has no design but the ones we invent. If *we* are the highest minds, the only meanings are the ones we create.

FREUD: Precisely.

SOCRATES: So once again, it seems that atheism is *the unproved premise* of your entire investigation.

FREUD: I do not agree that it is unproved. I believe I have explained religion as an illusion quite rationally and convincingly.

SOCRATES: In other words, you give a psychological explanation of theism rather than a logical proof for atheism.

FREUD: Yes.

SOCRATES: But a religious believer could equally give a psychological explanation of your atheism. In fact, he could use your own principles in doing that—the Oedipus complex, for instance. You yourself had a classically "Freudian" relationship with your father.

FREUD: We go back to the fit between the hand and the glove, then. Religion and human desires correspond so nicely that either God created man in His own image or we created Him in ours. I explain very well why it is the latter.

SOCRATES: But the theist can psychoanalyze you as much as you can psychoanalyze him. Such psychological arguments go nowhere, for they cancel each other out, leaving the objective question remaining, like a survivor of a battle in which both sides destroy each other. For *whatever* someone says, whatever the content of his philosophy, atheist or theist or anything else, you can always impugn his motives. You can always ask him "why" he believes it, meaning not the logical "why" but the psychological "why." And however convincing your impugning of his motives may be, that is still not a refutation of his content. For instance, even if you could prove that Newton's motives for propounding his law of gravity were simply to gain fame, or money, or the attention of a woman, that would not disprove the law itself.

FREUD: That's the difference between your enterprise and mine, Socrates; between logic and psychology. You claim to prove things with certainty. I don't.

SOCRATES: But neither one of our two different enterprises disproves the other.

FREUD: I quite agree.

SOCRATES: So you do not disprove religion by showing that its psychological origin is infantile fear—even if you did show that. Remember my example of Newton.

FREUD: I do not claim to "prove" or "disprove" things in your sense, Socrates, because I do not make the claims for reason that you make. I do not claim that human reason can know objective and universal truths, especially about values. Frankly, that claim seems to me to be preposterously pretentious, in fact the origin of many other harmful pretensions. And many philosophies seem to me to be almost as blameworthy as religions in that way.

SOCRATES: But you do yourself use reason to investigate human thoughts and behaviors.

FREUD: Yes. The tool is weak, but it's all we have. It's at least stronger than religious faith, or fears or fantasies or fallacies or fabrications, especially fundamentalisms.

SOCRATES: So many F-words! Such name-calling! So little logic! Well, let us return to our investigation of your text.

FREUD: It's about time.

SOCRATES: So for the rest of the book you will ask this revised and more modest question, the subjective rather than the objective question about life's meaning and value and purpose.

FREUD: Yes. I say: **We will therefore turn to the less ambitious question of what men themselves show by their behavior to be the purpose and intention of their lives. What do they demand of life and wish to achieve in it?**

SOCRATES: And then you immediately answer it by saying: **The answer to this can hardly be in doubt. They strive after happiness; they want to become happy and to remain so.** So you say that all men seek this end.

FREUD: Yes.

SOCRATES: So the answer is still universal, even though it is not objective.

FREUD: You may put it that way, yes. As even old Aristotle pointed out, there are three remarkable facts about happiness: *no* one prefers to be unhappy rather than happy, and *no* one seeks happiness as a mere means to any other end, and *everyone* seeks everything else as a means to this end, happiness.

SOCRATES: In other words, no one says "What good is happiness? It can't buy money." But some people say "What good is money? It can't buy happiness." And others say that it can.

FREUD: Yes.

SOCRATES: So you think you agree with Aristotle here.

FREUD: About happiness, yes.

SOCRATES: Do you think he meant the same thing by happiness as you did?

FREUD: Of course. Everyone knows what happiness is. It is what I say in the very next sentence: **This endeavour has two sides, a positive and a negative aim. It aims, on the one hand, at an absence of pain and unpleasure, and, on the other, at the experiencing of strong feelings of pleasure.**

SOCRATES: This is *not* an "of course." For Aristotle explicitly repudiated pleasure as the meaning of *human* happiness. For pleasure is not distinctively human, but shared with the irrational animals.

FREUD: But if happiness did not mean pleasure, then some men would find happiness in pain.

SOCRATES: And that seems impossible to you?

FREUD: Of course. Unless they are masochists, so that pain gives them pleasure.

SOCRATES: How then do you explain the fact that many men, like myself, who are not masochists, identify happiness with wisdom rather than pleasure, even though it comes only through pain and suffering?

FREUD: Perhaps you are a masochist.

SOCRATES: No, I do not say that pain itself is happiness, or that pleasure is unhappiness, only that pain is a lesser unhappiness than folly or vice; and that wisdom and virtue are a greater happiness than pleasure. And many believe this, for they would willingly sacrifice pleasures for wisdom, even accepting suffering as the price of wisdom.

FREUD: I think there are very few who live such an idealistic philosophy.

SOCRATES: Even if they do not practice it, they approve it and admire those who do. It's a common idea that it is necessary and good to learn wisdom through suffering. It's a very old and respected idea. Most ancient cultures believed it. Do you think it is simply nonsense?

FREUD: No, I think it's a case of sublimation. Lower and grosser and more obvious pleasures are given up for the sake of other, subtler pleasures which are thought to be higher, or finer.

SOCRATES: Like wisdom.

FREUD: Yes.

SOCRATES: And wisdom is thought to be higher because it is spiritual rather than physical.

FREUD: Yes.

SOCRATES: But *you* do not believe that. You are a materialist. You do not believe there are two distinct kinds of reality in man, spirit and matter.

FREUD: I do not.

SOCRATES: Then by what standard can we call pleasures like wisdom "higher" than sense pleasures?

FREUD: It is not I who make that claim, Socrates, but philosophers like you. I simply observe people's behavior. And one of the things that appears in all these observations is what I call "the pleasure principle."

SOCRATES: We must explore that next.

5.
Materialism and the Pleasure Principle

FREUD: I know what you will say about that, Socrates. You will quarrel with my scientific materialism, since you were not a materialist but an idealist: you believed in the superior reality of Platonic Ideas and in the reality of an immaterial soul and an immaterial god.

SOCRATES: You are wrong on all four counts. First, you do *not* know that. Second, your materialism is *not* scientific but metaphysical and philosophical. Third, I will *not* argue against it from the standpoint of any alternative philosophy, even my own. Fourth, it was Plato, not me, who taught the superior reality of the so-called Platonic Ideas. I was much more commonsensical.

FREUD: So you do not challenge my identification of reality with matter and of happiness with pleasure?

SOCRATES: I do indeed. But not in the name of an alternative metaphysical system, just in the name of logic and experience.

FREUD: Then I will win that challenge. For materialism is perfectly logical and perfectly in accord with experience.

SOCRATES: It is neither. It is not perfectly logical because it is self-contradictory. Materialism is not material. It is an ism, an idea. And it is not experiential because we experience immaterial things as well as material things: ideas as well as sensations, thinking subjects as well as thought objects.

FREUD: I don't understand why you say that materialism is *self-contradictory*.

SOCRATES: Because it is a philosophy, a thought. It is *a thought about* matter, is it not?

FREUD: Of course.

SOCRATES: But how can thoughts *about* matter be material?

FREUD: Why shouldn't they be?

SOCRATES: Thoughts are isms, not atoms.

FREUD: But if spiritualism is spiritual and alcoholism is alcoholic, why is materialism not material?

SOCRATES: Because you say materialism is a *true* thought, do you not? And immaterialism an untrue thought?

FREUD: Yes.

SOCRATES: So you grant the reality of truth.

FREUD: Yes, but truth is not a thing, but only a relationship between some thoughts and things. Do you disagree with that?

SOCRATES: No, I agree. And would you call it a relationship of *correspondence*, or matching, or imaging of some kind?

FREUD: Yes.

SOCRATES: That is indeed the commonsensical notion of the meaning of the word. Let us accept that. Now I ask you: How can truth—the relationship of some kind of correspondence between thoughts and things—be itself a material thing? How can the relationship between A and B be either A or B rather than something other than both? Saying that thoughts are only a strange kind of things seems to be as impossible as saying that things are only a strange kind of thoughts.

FREUD: I think I see your logical point, although just barely. It is very abstract. Perhaps you are right. But even so, that argument may be valid against simple, hard-line materialism, but I am not a simple, hard-line materialist. I distinguish mind and body, psyche and soma. I grant the existence of mental activity.

SOCRATES: So you admit that thoughts exist.

FREUD: Of course they exist. They occur.

SOCRATES: And thought is not composed of atoms. You can't say that a true thought, like "2+2=4" or "the sky is blue" has more atoms in it, or fewer atoms in it, than a false thought, like "2+2=5" or "the sky is green."

FREUD: Of course not. But its *causes* are composed of atoms. I trace that causes of thought to physical and chemical activity.

SOCRATES: So you are an epiphenomenalist.

FREUD: What is that?

SOCRATES: You reduce thought to an epiphenomenon.

FREUD: What is an epiphenomenon?

SOCRATES: An immaterial phenomenon—something mental or emotional—which appears only as the effect of a material phenomenon.

FREUD: Yes. That is what I say. Physics and chemistry can account for thought. Thought does not have the same kind of independent power to cause other things that material causes have.

SOCRATES: So it is an effect, not a cause.

FREUD: Ultimately, yes.

SOCRATES: So the thought that I want to raise my arm is not the cause of my arm being raised?

FREUD: Of course it is. But that thought, in turn, has material causes. You can't think without a brain and a body. That's why I said that *ultimately* matter is the cause. But matter can produce not only more matter but also thought, which can then affect material events in the body.

SOCRATES: But ultimately, it is always material things that cause immaterial things. Visible things cause invisible things.

FREUD: Yes.

SOCRATES: Like the trees causing the wind.

FREUD: You can't argue from an analogy.

SOCRATES: I know that. I'm not trying to argue, just trying to understand. Let's use another analogy. You say that thought is something like the puff of smoke that comes from a steam engine's chimney. It does not move the engine, but the engine moves it. It results from material pressures inside the engine.

FREUD: Yes.

SOCRATES: Like a fart.

FREUD: There is no need to be vulgar.

SOCRATES: It is your philosophy that is vulgar, I think. For you are saying that thought is only a sort of fart of the brain.

FREUD: I repeat: There is no need to be vulgar.

SOCRATES: But there is a need to be accurate. And that is an accurate analogy, except that thoughts do not smell—except perhaps in a metaphorical way.

FREUD: Look here, Socrates, I thought we were supposed to be examining my book rather than my metaphysics. You have changed our playing field from mine to yours, from my practical and psychological book to your theoretical and metaphysical principles, from something concrete that I did in fact write and now hold in my hands, to something abstract.

SOCRATES: I am guilty as charged. I confess and repent, and return to your actual text.

FREUD: Thank you.

SOCRATES: The reason I asked you about materialism was that it is not merely an abstract and impersonal theory in metaphysics but the premise for your very practical and personal "pleasure principle." And here is what you say about that:

> **As we see, what decides the purpose of life is simply the programme of the pleasure principle. This principle dominates the operation of the mental apparatus from the start. There can be no doubt about its efficacy . . .**

I wonder whether you mean by that merely that "there can be no doubt" that it is *a* powerful motive for *many* of our actions, or that "there can be no doubt" that it is *the* motive for *all* of our actions?

FREUD: All of them.

SOCRATES: Including our choice to speak as we do?

FREUD: Of course.

SOCRATES: So it is pleasure rather than truth that motivates us when we speak.

FREUD: Yes. But it can be both.

SOCRATES: But the reason we seek truth is that it gives us a kind of pleasure.

FREUD: Yes.

SOCRATES: So there is nothing higher or greater or stronger than pleasure by which we can judge it and curb it.

FREUD: There is nothing *stronger,* but I do not deny that we can and do judge pleasures by so-called "higher" *standards.* We can reject a pleasure because we calculate that it would result in too great a pain. That would be using an intellectual standard to judge pleasures, by a kind of calculation of results.

SOCRATES: And we often use moral standards too, don't we? Suppose it would give me great pleasure to steal a fortune, and suppose I believe I could get away with it without being punished, without suffering too great a pain. I might still not do it simply because I believe it is unjust, unfair.

FREUD: We do often act that way, yes; but even then

the pleasure principle is working. For we believe that it would give us greater pleasure to think of ourselves as morally good persons than to steal the fortune and know we are robbers. I do not deny that the pains of conscience can sometimes deter us more powerfully than the pains of poverty.

SOCRATES: But you say that the reason we do that is that it gives us pleasure to do it.

FREUD: Yes. The Germans have a saying: "A good conscience is your best pillow."

SOCRATES: So moral conscience is merely a pleasant sleeping pill?

FREUD: No. More often, it is a pleasant waking pill.

SOCRATES: But it is always pleasure that is our first mover.

FREUD: Yes.

SOCRATES: Not morality.

FREUD: No.

SOCRATES: Or even reason as such, the sheer thirst for truth, as distinct from the practical calculation of pleasures.

FREUD: That is what I say.

SOCRATES: So then all reasoning is really rationalizing of desire—the desire for pleasure.

FREUD: My experience and research with human motivations has convinced me that that is in fact the way it is. That is my "pleasure principle."

SOCRATES: And that applies to *all* the actions, and *all* the words of *all* persons at *all* times?

FREUD: Yes.

SOCRATES: Including you, then, when you announce that principle?

FREUD: Yes.

SOCRATES: So if it gave you more pleasure to lie to me, you would lie to me.

FREUD: Yes. But it doesn't.

SOCRATES: So the reason you teach me this "pleasure principle" of yours, ultimately, in the last analysis, is that it gives you pleasure?

FREUD: Yes. But I have been trained to take pleasure in learning and teaching truth.

SOCRATES: But it is pleasure that determines truth rather than truth that determines pleasure?

FREUD: I put it in psychological terms, not metaphysical terms: it is *desire* that determines *belief* rather than belief that determines desire.

SOCRATES: The desire for pleasure determines our beliefs about truth?

FREUD: Yes.

SOCRATES: Even for you, when you state that principle?

FREUD: Yes.

SOCRATES: Why then should I believe it? Especially if it does not give *me* pleasure?

FREUD: Because it is also true, and if truth gives you pleasure it can give you pleasure. We can be motivated by both. It gives me pleasure to discover truths in my scientific explorations, and to teach them, and it gives you pleasure to learn the truths that others discover and teach, doesn't it?

SOCRATES: It does. But you say that it is pleasure that is our final end rather than truth, don't you? You say that deep down, and in the long run, we all choose truth for pleasure, not pleasure for truth.

FREUD: Yes.

SOCRATES: And this principle is true of all men?

FREUD: Yes.

SOCRATES: And therefore it is true for your readers as well as for yourself?

FREUD: Of course.

SOCRATES: Do you also then appeal to the pleasure principle on the part of your readers, as *their* deepest motive?

FREUD: I must, since this is the deepest motive of all men.

SOCRATES: So your underlying message to all of us, in all that you say, is *not*: "Believe this because it is true" but "Believe this because it gives you pleasure."

FREUD: This is not my logical argument, but that is my readers' subconscious motive. On the deepest level, pleasure is always the motive.

SOCRATES: But if that is the case, then if your philosophy does *not* give me pleasure I have no reason to believe it—in fact I *cannot* believe it. If I am distressed rather than comforted by your materialism and your atheism and your reductionism and your hedonism and your pessimism, then I cannot believe it.

FREUD: You may still have *reasons* to believe it—I provide very good scientific evidence for what I say—but you will not have the *motive* to believe it if you think it will cause you more pain to believe it than to disbelieve it.

I am surprised at you, Socrates. You are confusing motives with reasons. Motives move us. They happen. They are efficient causes. Reasons are like blueprints; they merely define, they do not move. They do not *happen.*

You are forgetting your own distinction—or perhaps it was Aristotle's—between the efficient cause and the final cause, the origin and the end, the moving cause and the ideal. I say that pleasure is always the efficient cause; I do not say it is always the final cause, at least on the conscious level. We can have other conscious ends than pleasure.

SOCRATES: Aristotle distinguished *four* causes. You mentioned only two. What about the material cause and the formal cause—that out of which a thing is made and that into which a thing is made?

FREUD: I think the four really come down to two. I think this distinction I just used, between the efficient cause and the final cause, is really the same as the one between the material cause and the formal cause, because I believe that efficient causes are always material. It is only ideals, or ends, or final causes, that are immaterial forms or patterns—things like justice, or beauty.

SOCRATES: I do not agree with your reducing the four causes to two, but I am willing to argue in your terms rather than in mine. In terms of your distinction, then, between the two kinds of causes, would you not say that we have an obligation to let the formal and final cause determine the material and efficient cause; to let the specifying reason determine the moving cause; in other words to act according to reason? *Shouldn't* I be honest and believe an idea just because it is true, rather than following the pleasure principle and believing whatever ultimately gives me the most pleasure? How can science progress unless scientists are honest?

FREUD: That is a good rule to follow, of course.

SOCRATES: So you agree that we have a moral obligation to be honest?

FREUD: I'm not sure what you mean by a "moral obligation." I sense some absolute rearing its ugly head.

SOCRATES: But you will admit that it's *good* to be honest, at least, won't you? At least because science and progress depend upon it?

FREUD: Indeed. But that is not an absolute, that is pragmatic.

SOCRATES: But for that pragmatic reason, at least, we *should* be honest?

FREUD: Yes, of course.

SOCRATES: Then in your thinking isn't there a terrible, tragic conflict at the very heart of human nature between these two goods or desirable things? Between what we all *should* do—be honest—and what we all *have* to do, according to you, namely follow the pleasure principle?

FREUD: I do not claim to tell you what you *should* believe, or what you should do. I do not philosophize about that, as you do. I only tell you what you *will* believe, what will in fact motivate your beliefs, and what will motivate every other choice and action of yours. And that is in fact the pleasure principle. You philosophize about the formal and final cause, I philosophize about the material and efficient cause. I'm like Galileo: he told the bishops who confused theology with astronomy that they could tell him how to go to heaven but he would tell them how the heavens go.

SOCRATES: I agree with your distinction, but surely the two things we are distinguishing ought to be brought into the right relationship, like a happy marriage, shouldn't they, instead of just being divorced?

FREUD: That's a philosophical question. It's abstract, idealistic, and theoretical. That's for you to answer, not for me.

SOCRATES: Then let me translate it into a concrete, practical, and personal question. Don't you believe that there is a moral obligation for us to seek the truth even if the truth would bring us pain while a lie would bring us pleasure? Don't you believe in honesty?

FREUD: Of course I do. I am not an immoralist. I do not defend lying. But that is not my message in this book. I am a psychologist, not a moralist.

SOCRATES: You are a human being, are you not?

FREUD: Of course.

SOCRATES: Then you are a moralist. Everyone is a moralist. It's part of human nature.

FREUD: So I am a moralist. So what follows from that?

SOCRATES: Do you believe that honesty is a moral obligation?

FREUD: Insofar as anything is a moral obligation, I suppose honesty is, yes.

SOCRATES: And do you believe that honesty is a moral obligation only for psychologists, or only for scientists, or only for philosophers, or for all men?

FREUD: For all men, of course. For a very practical reason. How could society progress if we did not trust each other to be honest?

SOCRATES: But this is something no one can ever do, according to your psychology! No one can act contrary to the pleasure principle, you said.

FREUD: That's right.

SOCRATES: So you are saying that we all have a moral obligation to do what it is absolutely impossible for any of us to do at any time, namely to seek the truth even if it gives us pain instead of pleasure. What a strange morality that is! We *ought* to do what you say we *cannot* do. You disagree, then, with Kant's principle that "'ought implies 'can.'"

FREUD: I probably should not have called it a moral *obligation*. It is an *ideal* which we cannot reach perfectly, but we can get closer to it, we can approximate it.

SOCRATES: How can we even approximate it? How can we ever subject pleasure to truth? How can we ever contradict the pleasure principle?

FREUD: We can't. But *within,* or *under,* the pleasure principle we can still seek truth. We can unite truth and pleasure. We can find pleasure in truth instead of in falsehood. That is what you yourself taught in the

"Republic," Socrates—or perhaps it was your pupil Plato—when you said that children should be taught to like, and find pleasure in, beautiful sounds and sights and bodies, so that they would be thus conditioned to find pleasure in higher beauties, in beauties of soul and character, in wisdom and virtue, when they matured.

SOCRATES: But how can we do that instruction if you are right about your pleasure principle?

FREUD: Why not? This way of learning seems perfectly compatible with my principle.

SOCRATES: Perhaps learning is, but teaching is not.

FREUD: Why not?

SOCRATES: Because the teacher appeals to a higher principle, and subjects pleasure to truth in choosing which things he will teach his pupils to take pleasure in. But this subjecting of pleasure to truth is something you say none of us can do.

FREUD: We *can* do it. It is just conditioning. And we can pass it on if we have ourselves been conditioned to it by our own teachers when we were malleable youths.

SOCRATES: But this merely passes the buck, so to speak. Where does it begin? How could the first teacher ever have contradicted the pleasure principle in subjecting pleasures to the rule of reason and truth so that he could pass it on to others?

FREUD: An interesting question. Highly theoretical.

SOCRATES: It must begin somewhere, since it happens.

FREUD: True.

SOCRATES: Now if it began in a god, it would be possible, for a god does not have to learn as a child from others. But you say there are no gods.

FREUD: Indeed not.

SOCRATES: In fact, you trace everything human to something less than human, by evolution, rather than to something more than human, don't you?

FREUD: I do. That's scientific, both in biology and in general. Progress: that's how things happen: they evolve from below rather than descend from above.

SOCRATES: I don't see how that can possibly be "scientific," since it seems to violate the basic law of all scientific explanation, the principle of causality: that effects require adequate causes; that nothing can give what it does not have; that something cannot come from nothing and more cannot come from less.

FREUD: Great oaks come from little acorns, Socrates.

SOCRATES: But those little acorns do not just happen; they come from great oaks, as eggs come from chickens as well as chickens from eggs.

FREUD: I suppose you, as an absolutist, would say that the chicken comes before the egg?

SOCRATES: Yes. I would say that the egg is for the chicken before the chicken is for the egg. And you, as a relativist, would say that it is just as correct to say that a chicken is only one egg's clever way of making more eggs?

FREUD: Again we have descended into abstract metaphysical arguments instead of exploring what I actually said in my book.

SOCRATES: I did not realize that eggs and chickens were abstract. The one I ate today seemed quite concrete.

FREUD: I thought we were supposed to be exploring what I said in my book.

SOCRATES: But we *are* exploring something you said in your book, namely that there can be no doubt about the efficacy of the pleasure principle. And you have not yet answered my simple question: If the pleasure principle is absolute, how can we judge pleasure by truth or reason or goodness? If the truth gives us pain, how can we make it give us pleasure instead? For if we can't do that, how can we choose truth?

FREUD: That is a question for another book. The argument of this one does not depend on which one of us is right about the relationship between pleasure and truth. Even if we dropped this sentence, which you question, my argument would proceed unabated.

SOCRATES: Let us then proceed unabated through your argument.

FREUD: Thank you. I continue, speaking of the pleasure principle,

There can be no doubt about its efficacy, and yet its programme is at loggerheads with the whole world, with the macrocosm as much as with the microcosm. There is no possibility at all of its being carried through; all the regulations of the universe run counter to it. One feels inclined to say that the intention that man should be "happy" is not included in the plan of "Creation."

SOCRATES: As one great writer said, "If man were born to be happy, he would not be born to die."

FREUD: A good argument. Was that Epicurus, perhaps? An atheist like myself, no doubt.

SOCRATES: Actually it was the greatest religious novelist of the 20th century, Solzhenitsyn.

FREUD: Oh. I thought traditional religious thinkers like Aristotle and Aquinas said that we *were* born to be happy, that happiness was the ultimate end.

SOCRATES: But they meant by "happiness" something very different than what you meant. They meant something that included suffering and often martyrdom.

FREUD: That hardly sounds like happiness to me.

SOCRATES: Indeed. Your next sentence explains what you mean by happiness, and it is something subjective: if you feel happy, you are happy, and if you don't, you're not, and that's the end of it. And not only that, but it's also something material rather than spiritual. And not only that, but also something that is merely temporary and can never be permanent. You say:

What we call happiness in the strictest sense comes from the (preferably sudden) satisfaction of needs which have been dammed up to a high degree, and it is from its nature only possible as an episodic phenomenon.

You seem to take sexual orgasm as the prototype and standard of all happiness. Indeed, you explicitly say that a little later in the book. I wonder how you would explain the happiness of saints, monks, and old people, all of whom are on average notably happier than others, yet without orgasms. In fact, the people who experience the most orgasms, the so-called "sexually active," are on average the most unhappy, the most prone to depression, violence, and suicide.

FREUD: So *you* say, Socrates.

SOCRATES: No, so statistical surveys show, quite dramatically. But let us not linger over that sidebar. You next say, essentially, that happiness, at least the only kind you can imagine, is *boring:*

When any situation that is desired by the pleasure principle is prolonged, it only produces a feeling of mild contentment. We are so made that we can derive intense enjoyment only from a contrast and very little from a state of things.

Surely this is true only of shallow, foolish, and immature people? Surely the wiser and better we are, the more and deeper contentment we find in the permanent things, the ordinary things? Surely it is the addict who has to constantly increase his dosage to increase his "high"?

FREUD: We can learn a lot about ourselves from addicts, Socrates. We can learn to "know thyself."

SOCRATES: I do not doubt that. But is that all we are?

FREUD: No. But that is one of the things we are.

SOCRATES: So we are all pleasure addicts.

FREUD: Indeed.

SOCRATES: But how can we judge and pity our addictions if we have no higher self to sit in that judge's bench? And how can we overcome them if we cannot judge them?

6.
Changing the Question Again: From the Question about Happiness to the Question about Unhappiness

FREUD: I don't like where you are leading this argument, Socrates. I fear you are about to lead us into an abstract philosophical issue about the so-called good and bad aspects of human nature. I thought you were supposed to be examining the main point of my book, the problem of unhappiness, or discontentment.

SOCRATES: You are quite right. Again I must repent of my digression. Back to your book.

You next say: **Unhappiness is much less difficult to experience.** You do believe, then, that most people are unhappy more often than they are happy?

FREUD: More *easily*, at least, yes.

SOCRATES: What a pity!

FREUD: But that is not my point, so I do not need to prove it.

SOCRATES: But it is your premise, your assumption, and your problem. But I will not argue that point now.

FREUD: Perhaps you should. I would rather be argued with than pitied.

SOCRATES: But as you say, we are here to argue and examine your book.

You go on to dissect the sources of unhappiness with great precision, I think, when you say:

We are threatened with suffering from three directions:

from our own body, which is doomed to decay and dissolution and which cannot do without pain and anxiety as warning signals;

from the external world, which may rage against us with overwhelming and merciless forces of destruction;

and finally from our relations to other men. The suffering which comes from this last source is perhaps more painful to us than any other.

FREUD: "With great precision," you say. How surprising! A word of praise from you.

SOCRATES: I always praise the truth. And indeed what you say here is true, especially your last sentence. And I think that is because the *joy* that comes to us from this source is also greater than the joy that comes from the other two sources. We are happier if we are poor and old but in love than we are when we are rich and young but divorced.

FREUD: We see the same data, at least, even though I think we interpret it through different lenses.

SOCRATES: And I think your pessimistic lenses move you to change the main question of your book a second time, to a question with less hope, less optimism. The first time, you changed it from an objective and absolute question—"**what *is* of true value in life?**"—to a subjective and relative question—"**what do men show by their behaviour to be the purpose and intention of *their* lives?**" And now you change it a second time, from "How can we attain the most happiness?" to "How can we escape the most unhappiness and suffering?" For you next say:

It is no wonder if, under the pressure of these possibilities of suffering, men are accustomed to moderate their claims to happiness—just as the pleasure principle itself, indeed, under the influence of the external world, changed into the more modest reality principle—if a man thinks himself happy merely to have escaped unhappiness or to have survived his suffering.

FREUD: What faults do you find with my logic here?

SOCRATES: None—though if I were a psychologist I would find fault with your pessimism or lack of hope. Your philosophy sounds exactly like the view of a seriously depressed person. But that is not my expertise, so I am ready to explore the seven answers to your question that you consider next.

FREUD: So am I.

7.
The "Most Effective Method"

SOCRATES: I have examined many philosophers and their writings, and nearly all of them give some answer to the most important of all questions, the question you ask at the beginning of this book, "What is of true value in life?" or "What is the meaning, end, or purpose or life?" or "What is the greatest good, the 'summum bonum'?"—whether in this original, simple form, or in the doubly amended form that you prefer. And I have found six of your seven answers in many other philosophers, but never the seventh answer, which you give not last but first, and which you say is "**the most effective**" of all. Some of these other philosophers, like you, dismiss the other six answers as inadequate, while others embrace one of them. I am not shocked by any of their answers, but I am shocked by yours. I do not exaggerate when I say that with regard to this single most important question in the world, I find your answer the most shocking one I have ever heard.

FREUD: *I* am shocked to hear you say that, Socrates.

SOCRATES: Why?

FREUD: Because nearly everyone, including that paragon of common sense, Aristotle, says the same thing I say: that we all seek *happiness* as the final end.

SOCRATES: Oh, *that* is not what is shocking to me. Nearly everyone agrees with that, except Kant and the Stoics. (And even some of *them* speak of happiness.) It is the next question—what *is* happiness, what is the content of happiness, what is it that makes us happy?—that you answer so shockingly. You answer is unique among famous thinkers.

FREUD: That is not true either. For many other philosophers, though not all, say what I say, that happiness means pleasure. They are called Hedonists. Epicurus, Hobbes, Hume, and Mill could all be classified along with me as Hedonists. I am not the only one who believes that happiness means pleasure both in fact and also for most of mankind.

Nor am I the only materialist. Many other philosophers, and not just the four I mentioned, believe along with me that there is no such thing as a separate substance called the spiritual soul, a kind of little god, which seeks radically different things than pleasure and which should be followed and satisfied even at the expense of supposedly "lower" material goods. Hedonism is a fairly common philosophy. I do not see why you are shocked by it. It is the theory of value that logically follows materialism as a theory of reality, a metaphysic.

SOCRATES: It is indeed. I do not find hedonism or materialism shocking. But I think you are shocking because you follow out the logical implications of this materialism and hedonism more consistently than any other philosopher. I compliment you on this. You logically deduce your shocking practical answer to the question of what is life's highest value, or the most effective method of solving its fundamental problem, the problem of unhappiness, or unpleasure, from the premise of materialism (which is indeed, as you say, fairly common among philosophers, especially in your modern era). Yet none of these other philosophers embraced your answer, though I think it logically follows from their premises.

Let me read your two sentences that express first this theoretical premise and then this practical conclusion with wonderful simplicity and directness. The second comes immediately after the first because it is the conclusion that follows from the premise.

I am a little bit afraid to do this, because I fear that some people may actually embrace your absurd conclusion as the logical result of your apparently respectable premise, rather than rejecting your premise as the logically necessary price for rejecting your conclusion. In other words, your conclusion, it seems to me, is so absurd that it refutes your premise: a classic example of a *reductio ad absurdum* argument.

Here are the two sentences:

In the last analysis, all suffering is nothing else than sensation; it only exists insofar as we feel it, and we only feel it in consequence of certain ways in which our organism is regulated.

The crudest, but also the most effective among these methods of influence is the chemical one—intoxication.

So in a word your best answer to life's deepest problem is—drugs!

FREUD: I do not unqualifiedly recommend to everyone to use drugs, Socrates. I experimented with cocaine myself, and know something of its dangers and addictions first hand, as well as its powers. This is why I say, later in that very paragraph, that **one knows that, with**

the help of this "downer of cares" one can at any time withdraw from the pressure of reality and find refuge in a world of one's own with better conditions of sensibility. As is well known, it is precisely this property of intoxicants which also determines their danger and their injuriousness.

SOCRATES: But this "injuriousness," to you, is merely that **They are responsible, in certain circumstances, for the useless waste of a large quota of energy which might have been employed for the improvement of the human lot.** So if a drug could be found that had no such "injuriousness," no such bad side effects—a drug like "soma" in *Brave New World*—then this would be your answer to life's deepest problem.

FREUD: I do not see how such a drug could be possible. All known drugs—

SOCRATES: Then you have a very limited scientific imagination.

FREUD: Look here, Socrates, it is irrational for you to be shocked at what I say, for you yourself admit that it logically follows from my premises. If, in the first place, the thing that we all hate and fear the most is unhappiness, misery, and pain; and if, in the second place, this is a sensation, and not some purely spiritual thing like "sin" or "alienation from God" or even mere ignorance, as you and Plato probably would say; and if, in the third place, like all sensations it exists only insofar as we feel it; and if, in the fourth place, we feel it only in consequence of the ways our physical and chemical organism is regulated; and if, in the fifth place, a drug can change that way, that regulation, that influence—why, then, there is no weak link in that chain of argument. The conclusion follows with logical necessity.

SOCRATES: Oh, I wholly agree with you about that!

FREUD: You do?

SOCRATES: Yes! That is why I said your argument was a "reductio ad absurdum." You have had the courage and the logical consistency to deduce the practical consequences of your premise of materialism. No other materialistic philosopher has been that courageously logical.

FREUD: I am surprised by your compliment. I thought I was being insulted rather than complimented.

SOCRATES: Oh, you are being insulted too. For you do not realize that you have undermined the faith of most of your fellow materialists by this argument.

FREUD: Don't you think I have persuaded them to accept my conclusion instead?

SOCRATES: Well, perhaps you have. That is indeed the danger of being so logically consistent. To determine which outcome is the more likely—accepting your absurd conclusion that a drug like soma would be the most effective solution to life's fundamental problem, or rejecting your materialistic premise that leads logically to that conclusion—we have to ask the next question, which is the only remaining question. For, once we have established this unbreakable chain between your metaphysical premise and your practical conclusion, the only remaining question, which will decide whether to embrace both your premise and your conclusion or to reject both of them—for they are a "package deal"—is this: which of these two things is more certain? That drugs are a really stupid answer to life's deepest problem, and that therefore your materialistic premise is false? Or that materialism is true, that there is no such thing as an invisible soul or spirit or God, either within us or without, so that your conclusion about drugs, which follows from this premise, is also true? Which of these two things do we know to be true by experience and which of them is a faith, an ideology, a mere opinion?

FREUD: Do you actually believe that my argument will persuade many materialists to abandon their materialism?

SOCRATES: I hope so. But perhaps I am wrong. Perhaps I have too much confidence in mankind's willingness to follow the logic of an argument wherever it leads. Perhaps most readers will cling to their faith, their ideology, even in the teeth of both logic and experience. Like John the Boy Who Thought He Was Dead.

FREUD: Who is that?

SOCRATES: Oh, just a character in a story. Would you like to hear it? It's about a psychiatrist.

FREUD: I suspect I have no choice. In any case, I am curious. So tell your story.

SOCRATES: John was brilliant in every way but he had this one very strange belief: he believed he was dead. Nothing anyone could do could dissuade him. His parents despaired of a cure until they found a psychiatrist who guaranteed that he could cure John of this delusion. But the price was steep: $250,000. But nothing else worked, and finally, John's parents agreed.

They paid the psychiatrist his fee, and he used the money to send John to medical school for four years. When John graduated, the psychiatrist told John and his parents to come to his office for the cure. They came, and this is the conversation that cured him:

"John," the psychiatrist said, "you learned everything everyone else learned at medical school, did you not? And you got straight As in all your subjects, did you not?"

"I did," said John.

"You took Anatomy and Physiology, did you not?"

"Yes. And I got an A."

"I'd like to ask you one question then. Do dead men bleed?"

"Only for a few minutes," John said.

"But not after they have been dead for 25 years?"

"No. That's impossible."

"How old are you, John?"

"Twenty five."

"Thank you. Now I have a second question for you. You learned scientific method, did you not? Especially as it applies to medical practice?"

"Yes."

"So you learned that an essential step is careful observation, did you not?"

"Yes."

"Now I'm going to perform a little experiment, John, and I want you to observe it very carefully and tell me what presents here." The doctor took a pin and pricked John's hand. It started to bleed. "What do you see, John?"

"I'm bleeding."

"Very good, John. Now just one more question. You took a course in Logic, did you not? And you got a straight A in that too, did you not?

"Yes."

"Now I want you to put your answers to my first two questions together as two premises, and draw the logical conclusion from them."

"Oh, my goodness! Doctor, I have been a fool all my life. You've cured me of my illusion. Dead men bleed after all."

FREUD: Very funny, to a logician, I'm sure. And the parallel between John and myself is . . . ?

SOCRATES: You both cling to an ideology and deny the data of experience instead of doubting the ideology when experience contradicts it.

FREUD: I don't see the parallel at all. What is the ideology and what is the experience?

SOCRATES: With John, the ideology was the belief that he was dead, and the experience was that dead men do not bleed. With you, the ideology is materialism, and the experience is that drugs are NOT the best answer to the problem of happiness.

FREUD: A rather far-fetched analogy, I think. Besides, analogies prove nothing.

SOCRATES: Neither does the sight of blood—to one whose mind is already made up.

But it is time for us to explore your six other answers to the question of the "summum bonum."

8. Mysticism and Yoga

SOCRATES: The next solution you explore, after this crude and material one, is a subtle, spiritual one:

The complicated structure of our mental apparatus admits, however, of a whole number of other influences. Just as a satisfaction of an instinct spells happiness for us, so severe suffering is caused us if the external world lets us starve, if it refuses to sate our needs. One may therefore hope to be freed from a part of one's sufferings by influencing the instinctual impulses. This type of defense is no longer brought to bear on the sensory apparatus; it seeks to master the internal sources of our needs. The extreme form of this is brought about by killing off the instincts, as is prescribed by the worldly wisdom of the East and practiced by Yoga.

You mention yoga as an example of this second solution to the problem of pain, the psychical solution rather than the somatic one, is that correct?

FREUD: Yes.

SOCRATES: Yoga, of course, is a Hindu concept.

FREUD: Yes. But perhaps the clearest example of it is Buddhism, which recommends the denial of all desires, because, as Gotama the Buddha saw so simply and clearly, desires are a necessary condition for suffering. He called desires the fuel for the fire of suffering, and reasoned that if you cut off the fuel, the fire no longer burns.

SOCRATES: That sounds very logical.

FREUD: Yes. It is a kind of hypnosis which produces the same effect as drugs, but by a psychic rather than a somatic cause. Since pain is psychosomatic—since pain exists only in living persons with psyches and somas, not in ghosts or corpses—there are therefore two possibilities for ending pain: short-circuiting either the soma (which is what drugs do) or short-circuiting the psyche (which is what yoga does). Pain is like a message sent to the brain, and that message can be "shorted out" either by stopping it in its somatic dimension by drugs or in its psychic dimension by a kind of hypnosis.

SOCRATES: That also sounds very logical But why do you call this "**worldly wisdom**"? Hinduism and Buddhism are both mystical religions, or spiritualities.

FREUD: But their payoff is the relief of suffering. Although they do this by a mental causality—I have called them a kind of hypnosis—rather than the physical causality of chemical intoxication, I call them "worldly wisdom" because their end or payoff is not something otherworldly and contemplative—Heaven, or holiness, or Godliness—but something this-worldly and practical: the ending of suffering.

SOCRATES: I think most Hindus and Buddhists would disagree about that. They would not see the ultimate end of their religion as the conquest of *pain* but as a mystical "enlightenment," the conquest of *ignorance*.

FREUD: No, I think that is what *you* would say is the final end or greatest good, because you are an abstract, speculative philosopher. But most people are not. If you asked them what they were seeking above all, they would not say "knowledge" or "the conquest of ignorance" but "happiness," and "the conquest of suffering." I think you are projecting your own speculative, philosophical interests onto other men and other cultures. Even Aristotle agreed with me: he said that the end everyone always sought was happiness. And Buddha explicitly said that the fundamental problem of life was suffering. That was his "first noble truth": that life is suffering.

SOCRATES: Then perhaps we should identify this second solution of yours with Buddhism rather than Hindu yoga, since there is a version of yoga that is, like me, more speculative and intellectual: "jnana yoga," I believe, is what they call it.

FREUD: Whether it is Hindu or Buddhist is irrelevant, and whether it uses the intellect, like jnana yoga, or other powers, all forms of yoga aim at the "nirvana," the "extinction," of suffering.

SOCRATES: But they are *religions*. I do not understand why you call them "worldly wisdom."

FREUD: That's easy to see. Let's just take Buddhism, because it's the simplest and clearest version of yoga. (Most Hindus classify Buddhism as another form of yoga, by the way.)

Buddha summarized his entire philosophy in his "four noble truths," and when his disciples asked him to answer other, more theoretical questions, he refused to do so.

The "four noble truths" are perfectly practical. They correspond exactly to a medical analysis of a patient's condition who comes to the doctor for one reason only: to get rid of his pain.

Buddha's "first noble truth" is that all life is suffering, or *dukkha;* that to live is to suffer. This is the patient's complaint about his *symptoms.* They are the unwanted effects of a disease that causes them.

Buddha's "second noble truth" is that the cause of suffering is desire, or *tanha.* This is the doctor's *diagnosis* of the disease that is causing the symptoms: the unwanted cause of the unwanted effects.

Buddha's "third noble truth" is that to take away the cause is to take away the effect. This is the "extinction," or *nirvana,* of desire and therefore the extinction of suffering. It is the *prognosis* of the cure, or the healing—the healing from the symptoms by the healing of the disease. (All this assumes, of course, that desire is a *disease.*)

Buddha's "fourth noble truth" is that the way to extinguish desire, and thus suffering, is the "noble eightfold path" by which desire is gradually reduced to zero in each of life's eight distinguished areas. This corresponds to the *prescription* for the healing in the medical analogy.

Thus we have a combination of two variables: cause and effect, and wanted and unwanted. The symptoms are the unwanted effects, the disease is the unwanted cause, the prognosis is the wanted effect, and the prescription is the wanted cause. What is most remarkable is that the unwanted, undesired cause, according to Buddha, is desire itself. So the Buddhist patient comes to his Buddhist doctor with a great *desire* for a cure, and is told that he must abolish *desire.*

SOCRATES: Your analysis of the Buddhist way is

remarkably clear and logical. What do you find lacking in this analysis of the human condition?

FREUD: The demonizing of desire. Buddhism is the elimination of passionate happiness and unhappiness alike by the elimination of passion. It is like spiritual euthanasia: killing the patient in order to cure the disease.

SOCRATES: I see. You mean by "the patient" the one who desires, and by "the disease" the pain that comes from desiring many things you do not get.

FREUD: Yes.

SOCRATES: And so you say that the Buddhist solution to suffering is not worth the price. You have to give up the sweets as well as the bitters?

FREUD: Exactly. As I say, **there is an undeniable diminution in the potentialities of enjoyment.**

SOCRATES: But if, as you believe, life contains more bitters than sweets, more pains than pleasures, then the abolition of both would be a progress, wouldn't it? It would be like a declaration of bankruptcy when the red ink overwhelms the black.

FREUD: In the abstract, yes. But I do not simply count the quantity of pleasures and pains, as the crude Utilitarians do. Like most men, I value the quality more than the quantity. And even a little pleasure counts more than a lot of pain if it is of great quality.

SOCRATES: What do you mean by "quality"?

FREUD: I mean intensity of passion, of course: the very thing yoga seeks to abolish, whether it is Hindu or

Buddhist. As I say, **The feeling of happiness derived from the satisfaction of a wild instinctual impulse untamed by the ego is incomparably more intense . . .**

SOCRATES: In other words, you are saying that no one would prefer silent, mystical contemplation to wild, screaming sex if he had the choice.

FREUD: To put it crudely, of course.

SOCRATES: Then how do you explain the data?

FREUD: What data?

SOCRATES: That those who have experienced both kinds of joy say the spiritual is greater, not the physical. Many mystics, like Augustine, once lived lives of passionate excitement, so they are in a good position to compare the two kinds of life. And therefore those who, like you, say that the physical is greater, those who rank physical over spiritual orgasm, must have never experienced the latter.

FREUD: Let me play Socrates to you, Socrates, and logically analyze just what you are saying here. You are saying to all of us who prefer the physical joys to the spiritual—which it seems to me are the great majority of men—that if we claim we have tasted both, and are thus in a position to compare them, and yet we rank the physical as greater than the spiritual, we must be either deceiving or deceived; either lying to you or lied to by our own minds and feelings. Does that not logically follow?

SOCRATES: It does indeed. You seem to have become infected by my habit of arguing logically about everything, even psychology.

FREUD: So which of the two do you call me, Socrates? A deliberate liar or one who is honest but deceived?

SOCRATES: The latter, I think.

FREUD: But it is not possible to be deceived by thinking you have enjoyed passionate sex when in fact you have not!

SOCRATES: But it *is* quite possible to be deceived by thinking that you have tasted true spiritual joys when in fact you have not. You may have tasted only a pale copy of them, a conventional imitation.

I do admit the main point of your criticism of yoga, though: that most men would not sacrifice their joys just to eliminate their sorrows. You speak of "**an undeniable diminishment in the potentialities of enjoyment**" if all desire is eliminated; and I think most men would agree with that. They accept suffering as the price for joy. In fact, that's the deal, so to speak—the deal that's made every time we *love* anyone or any thing. To give your heart to anything is to risk it being broken.

FREUD: Ah, yes, love. I have much more to say about that later. But let's take the candidates in order. You agree with my refutation of the yoga answer, though?

SOCRATES: I do.

9.
Art and Science

SOCRATES: Your next candidate is the creation of art and science, which is a more typically Western answer. Here is what you say about this candidate for the "summum bonum". . .

FREUD: Socrates, before you proceed, I want to register a protest against your putting me into the "summum bonum" game, so to speak; I mean pitting me against all those other philosophers who propose some attainable, adequate form of happiness. Remember, I am here in search of something more modest: not the attainment of the positive—happiness—but only the best reduction of the negative—suffering.

SOCRATES: I have not forgotten your cynicism about happiness—or, as you call it, your modesty: how low your ideals and hopes are.

FREUD: You are being ironic.

SOCRATES: Oh, thank you for enlightening me about that. I had forgotten my own intention.

FREUD: You are even ironic about being ironic! Do you really think it is appropriate to use personal insults when discussing such an important topic as this in a supposedly scientific and objective manner?

SOCRATES: If it is appropriate for you, it is appropriate for me.

FREUD: I have not insulted you.

SOCRATES: No, but you have insulted life itself, which is far more offensive. Socrates deserves many insults, but life does not.

FREUD: How have I insulted life?—assuming we can personify it in that way, as if it were a beautiful woman whom I have called ugly.

SOCRATES: That is exactly what you have done. You have insulted life by reducing the gift of life's "summum bonum" from the positive attainment of joy to the negative escape from suffering—exactly the mistake you rightly criticize in the defenders of yoga. The most you expect from life is what you expect from a garbage man, or an anaesthetist.

FREUD: Then why do I criticize yoga for sacrificing the passionate pleasure of satisfying "wild instinctual impulses"?

SOCRATES: Because you are logically inconsistent.

FREUD: If so, why do I not see that fact?

SOCRATES: Because you are not Socrates. You are Freud.

FREUD: More personal insult. Thank you so much, O totally objective and impersonal philosopher!

SOCRATES: But let us not argue about personal insults, whether to you or to me or to life. Let us do exactly what you call for: a scientific and objective investigation of your question.

FREUD: Thank you.

SOCRATES: Here, then, is what you say about your next candidate:

Another technique for fending off suffering is the employment of the displacements of libido which our mental apparatus permits of . . . Do you mean by "libido" *desires?*

FREUD: The psychic source and power of desires, yes. The instincts. Thus I say: **The task here is that of shifting the instinctual aims in such a way that they cannot come up against frustration from the external world . . .**

SOCRATES: This shift will be essentially the shift from material, bodily pleasures to mental or psychic ones—is that correct?

FREUD: That's correct. So I go on to say: **One gains the most if one can sufficiently heighten the yield of pleasure from the sources of psychical and intellectual work. When that is so, fate can do little against one.**

SOCRATES: You seem to assume here that fate rules the soma and the world of matter but not the psyche and the world of mind—and that sounds very much like the idea of free will. Am I mistaken to interpret you that way?

FREUD: Yes, you are wrong. I do not believe in free will.

SOCRATES: Does fate, then, rule everything for you?

FREUD: Yes.

SOCRATES: So you share the Stoics' world-view but not their practical conclusion about becoming passionless.

FREUD: You could say that, yes.

SOCRATES: And in this world view, both psyche and soma are ruled by fate?

FREUD: Yes.

SOCRATES: Then how can you say they are they different in kind and not just in degree?

FREUD: Because the way fate rules the external world is different in kind from the way it rules our inner life. We *seem,* to ourselves, at least, to have more control over the inner than over the outer workings of our lives. It does not matter whether we really do or not; we do not have to get into a philosophical argument about free will here. All that matters is that we *seem* to have such control, we *believe* it.

SOCRATES: Why do we believe it, if it is not true?

FREUD: For the same reason we do anything, including choosing our beliefs: because we think it will make us happier, or less unhappy.

SOCRATES: So we come back again to this foundational point: you say that we always seek pleasure, not truth, as our ultimate end.

FREUD: Yes—though the two may coincide.

SOCRATES: But when they do, we seek truth because it is pleasant, not pleasure because it is true?

FREUD: Yes.

SOCRATES: Always?

FREUD: Yes.

SOCRATES: Again I have to use the word "cynical" to label your position, though I fear you will take this as an insult against your person rather than your philosophy.

FREUD: Why do you call it "cynical?"

SOCRATES: Because you imply that truth and happiness, the two things everyone wants, often contradict each other; that we are made happier by illusions than by reality—whether these illusions are those of religion, or of intoxication, or of yoga, or of art and science, which is what you are considering in this passage.

FREUD: Yes.

SOCRATES: So even science is an illusion?

FREUD: No, but science's promise to make us happy is an illusion.

SOCRATES: How sad!

FREUD: As you must know, if you are indeed the inventor of logical argumentation, you cannot refute an idea by calling it a nasty name.

SOCRATES: I did not claim it was a refutation, only an accurate label.

But let us go on: You say: **A satisfaction of this kind, such as an artist's joy in creating, in giving his phantasies body, or a scientist's in solving problems or discovering truths, has a special quality . . .** By the way, I'm glad you at least acknowledge that the *kind* of pleasure or happiness or joy given to us by beauty and truth, and thus by art and science, has "a special quality," and not the same kind or quality as physical pleasures.

FREUD: Of course they are not the same.

SOCRATES: And in your very next words you confess that you cannot understand these spiritual joys by means of your materialistic psychology, so you take refuge in faith . . .

FREUD: *Faith?* I put no reliance on faith.

SOCRATES: Oh, but you do. In fact, you even call this faith "certain," even though it is not a faith in an actual, already-existing being such as God, but only in a potential, hoped-for future discovery by your materialistic psychological science. You say this satisfaction **has a special quality which we shall certainly one day be able to characterize in metapsychological terms. At present all we can say figuratively is that such satisfactions seem "finer" and "higher."** You have more faith in the future than religious believers have in the present. You have more faith in what you must admit is only a possibility than they have in what they claim is an actuality. And you have more faith in the human than they have in the divine.

It seems as if your contemporary G. K. Chesterton was right when he said that when people stop believing in God they do come to believe in nothing but in anything and everything. Religious believers do not claim that their knowledge of the spiritual will explain everything physical, with no remainder and no mystery left; but materialists like you claim that your knowledge of the material will one day explain everything spiritual, with no remainder and no mystery. You seem to have a far bigger faith than they do.

FREUD: But if there is no God, there is nothing else to put faith and hope in.

SOCRATES: And therefore I have to wonder whether you are actually a religious spy in the ranks of the atheists.

FREUD: I assume you are being ironic again. But why in the world would you say that, even in jest?

SOCRATES: Because what you said sounds very much like a "reductio ad absurdum" argument for the necessity of belief in God. Is it like the logic of Dostoyevsky's "if God does not exist, everything is permissible." The consequence is so absurd that it refutes the hypothesis.

That "reductio ad absurdum" strategy is also the logic of the cosmological argument, the "first cause" argument for God, as in Aquinas. It says that if there were no first cause, no Uncaused Cause, then there could not be any second causes, any caused causes. And to say there are no caused causes is absurd. Therefore atheism is refuted.

But those arguments—Dostoyevsky's moral argument and Aquinas's cosmological argument—are both overt in arguing for God, while your argument seems covert, like a spy's cover.

FREUD: I assure you, Socrates, that I am serious and sincere. I am not a spy.

SOCRATES: I will accept your protestation of innocence, even though that is exactly what I would expect from a good spy.

But once again this is a diversion. We should return to your overt argument.

FREUD: Thank you—again.

SOCRATES: Our next step is examining your refutation of art and science as adequate answers to life's problem of suffering. You say that although they do give a satisfaction of a special quality which you cannot yet explain (significantly, you do not even mention the words "beauty" or "truth"), the problem with them is that **their intensity is mild as compared with that derived from the sating of crude and primary instinctual impulses; it does not convulse our physical being.**

Clearly the touchstone and standard of comparison here, your "gold standard," is sexual orgasm. Art and science for you are weak answers to life's greatest problem because they "do not convulse our physical being." They are weak orgasms. I wonder whether you could find a single artist or scientist in the entire history of the world who would agree with you there. And if so, I wonder how scientific, how sensitive to your *data,* you are.

FREUD: That is an unfair oversimplification, Socrates. I did not use the word "orgasm," after all.

SOCRATES: Can you then tell me any other "sating of crude and primary instinctual impulses" that is delightful to us because it "convulses our physical being"? Are any other such physical convulsions pleasant to us? Vomiting, for instance? Or shaking with fear, or with the anger of vengeance?

FREUD: Hmph!

SOCRATES: Are your answers reduced to single animal-like syllables now?

FREUD: I have other objections as well, Socrates, besides the comparison with orgasms.

SOCRATES: This is true. For you say: **And the weak point of this method is that it is not applicable generally: it is accessible to only a few people. It**

presupposes the possession of special dispositions and gifts which are far from being common to any practical degree.

So you do not think that a child in elementary school, for instance, who lacks those special gifts which will make him one day a great artist or scientist, derives any real joy from solving a scientific puzzle that he thought was too difficult for him, or from painting a watercolor that for the first time actually looks like a willow tree, or a flying cardinal? Do you believe that only professional artists and scientists can find joy in truth or beauty? If you do *not* think that, why did you say it? And if you do believe it, how do you escape the charge of snobbery?

FREUD: It is obviously a matter of degree *how much* happiness art and science give to different people. But the most important objection to this method applies to everyone, both the great and the small. Look at what I say next: **And even to the few who do possess them, this method cannot give complete protection from suffering.**

SOCRATES: And you are clearly right here. For both the great and the small, achievement in these two fields not only does not protect one from suffering but actually *requires* suffering, at least the suffering of time and effort and frustration in failing many times to solve the scientific problem or to create the beauty intended. Most artists, in fact, are famous for saying that there is no great art without suffering. Our most beautiful music is in a minor key, and our most beautiful plays are tragedies.

FREUD: Why do you point out facts that prove my case rather than yours, Socrates?

SOCRATES: I have no "case." I am here merely to examine yours, not to defend another. And I point out these facts simply because they are true, and you are quite right here.

FREUD: Oh. I am surprised to hear you say that.

SOCRATES: But your being right here proves that you are wrong elsewhere.

FREUD: How? (How short that surprise was!)

SOCRATES: If it is true, as you say, that art and science do not effectively relieve suffering; and if it is further true, as I said, that everyone knows this in advance, by experience; and if it is also true, as we know by observation, that many people nevertheless enter and love and embrace these two enterprises—so much so that they are almost the signatures of civilization—and if, further, it is also true that everyone seeks happiness, as you also said, then it cannot be true that their motive for pursuing art and science is the one that you ascribe to them, namely the relief of suffering and the attainment of happiness or pleasure. Does that not logically follow?

FREUD: It seems to.

SOCRATES: Is it not clear, then, that people seek something else, something that I indicated with the common but mysterious words "beauty" and "truth," and that they deem these things so precious that for the sake of these things they will sacrifice pleasure and contentment, and knowingly embrace suffering?

FREUD: It seems so.

SOCRATES: And if this is so, that means that their

motives are much higher, more idealistic, more spiritual, than yours.

FREUD: So?

SOCRATES: So, therefore, correlatively, your motives are far lower, more cynical and more materialistic than theirs—that is, lower than those of nearly all of mankind.

FREUD: I have no scruples about contradicting "nearly all of mankind." Like you, Socrates, I upset popular opinions and expose popular pretensions.

SOCRATES: But if this is so, if you do not share or respect their ideals, or even understand them, if you do not understand how anyone could seek anything like beauty or truth as their ultimate end, then why should the rest of mankind take you, of all people, as their teacher about this thing, about the meaning of life, about human nature, about values, or even about your specialty, psychology, about human motivations? For if my logical analysis is correct, your theory of their motivations is a radical misunderstanding of both ordinary people and great artists and scientists. They believe they are seeking truth and beauty, and sacrificing pleasure for it; you say they are really only seeking to relieve pain.

FREUD: I do not merely reflect ordinary opinion, any more than you do, Socrates.

SOCRATES: But who, do you think, is more likely to be right about them and their motivations? Those who have the data or those who do not?

FREUD: What do you mean, "data"?

SOCRATES: You admit that all men seek pleasure and hate pain, do you not?

FREUD: Indeed.

SOCRATES: So all men experience this motivation.

FREUD: Yes.

SOCRATES: But most of them say they also experience other motivations—something they confusedly refer to by words like "truth" and "beauty." Do they not claim to experience this?

FREUD: They say that, yes.

SOCRATES: And whatever is immediately experienced is data to the experiencer, is it not?

FREUD: To him, yes. But he may be deceived.

SOCRATES: Who, do you think, is more likely to be deceived about the relationship between two things: one who experiences both of them or one who by his own confession experiences only one?

FREUD: You want me to say "The one who experiences less of the data," I suppose.

SOCRATES: But you do not believe that in this case, do you? For if you did, it would logically follow that *they* should be teaching *you* about the motivations toward truth and beauty, and about the relationship between this and the pleasure principle, rather than you teaching them.

FREUD: So what is your psychoanalysis of me now, Socrates? What do you claim I am really doing when I seem only to be scientifically analyzing these candidates for the relief of suffering?

SOCRATES: I think you are doing exactly what your own theory says that all men are always doing when they reason: you are rationalizing. In order to have the pleasure of maintaining your own hypothesis, you are impugning the data of the vast majority of the human race even though your hypothesis is confessedly based on only partial data.

FREUD: So what is your diagnosis, Doctor Socrates? How do you label my neurosis?

SOCRATES: The word "snobbery" comes to mind.

FREUD: "Sticks and stones may break my bones but names will never hurt me."

SOCRATES: I wasn't trying to hurt you.

FREUD: What were you trying to do?

SOCRATES: Examine you.

FREUD: If that ruthless kind of examination did not hurt people, why did they kill you for it?

SOCRATES: Because they were not wise enough to know that pain can be profitable, especially mental pain. Because they did not distinguish between wisdom and pleasure, or between needs and wants.

FREUD: So your task is to examine and question me, whether I want this or not, because I need it.

SOCRATES: That is correct.

FREUD: Why do I need it? Because I disagree with you?

SOCRATES: No. Because you apparently have not questioned yourself, and your own opinions, especially the ones which are so radically at odds with nearly universal human experience.

FREUD: But I have indeed questioned them, Socrates. I did not arrive at my opinions automatically or easily. The process was long and hard—and quite scientific, I might add.

SOCRATES: In that case I retract my personal insult. But if that is so, then as a scientist you *do* understand the sacrifices a scientist makes in his quest for the truth, and how this questing is *not* explained merely by the "pleasure principle," as you say everything is.

FREUD: I see the logical dilemma. So you think you've refuted me either way, don't you?

SOCRATES: No, I think you've refuted yourself.

10.
The Imagination

SOCRATES: But we need to explore your next candidate, the fourth one, which is the enjoyment, rather than the creation, of art. This is done by the creative imagination.

As I explore what you say about this, I have to apologize in advance for something.

FREUD: What?

SOCRATES: I'm afraid I will have to interrupt the flow of your writing many times.

FREUD: Why?

SOCRATES: Because I think that nearly everyone in the world would contradict what you say about it, both those who create the art and those who enjoy it.

FREUD: Why?

SOCRATES: Well, just look at what you say. You say the same thing of this candidate, the *enjoyment* of art, that you said about your last candidate, the *creation* of art (and science). You say:

While this procedure already clearly shows an intention of making oneself independent of the external world by seeking satisfaction in internal, psychical

processes, the next procedure brings out those features yet more strongly. In it, the connection with reality is still further loosened. Surely this is a very strange thing to say of science, at least, whose purpose is to know the external world and to control it, by technology.

FREUD: But I speak of the enjoyment in the process, not the result. And I say that that enjoyment is in the withdrawal from the external world that causes us so much suffering. Abstract scientific thinking is a kind of oasis in the desert of pain.

SOCRATES: So the real motive for science is the enjoyment of this oasis rather than the discovery of truth?

FREUD: Yes.

SOCRATES: Because a*ll* motives come under the pleasure principle?

FREUD: Yes.

SOCRATES: And the real pleasure comes in the process rather than the result?

FREUD: Yes. "It is better to travel hopefully than to arrive."

SOCRATES: But how could anyone ever travel hopefully if he did not hope to arrive?

FREUD: Clever wordplay, Socrates, but people do it.

SOCRATES: I suppose they do, but it must be a kind of intellectual contraception then.

FREUD: What in the world do you mean by that?

SOCRATES: In contraception, what we want is the

thrill of the process of sex, not its natural product, the baby. Is this not true?

FREUD: Yes. That is why I labeled it a perversion of a natural function.

SOCRATES: And we use contraceptives because we deem the thrill of the chase greater than the thrill of the chaste.

FREUD: Yes. We enjoy the process more than its natural result.

SOCRATES: So this is our motive for science: the enjoyment of the process of thinking?

FREUD: Yes.

SOCRATES: But the scientist does desire the baby of truth, and welcomes it when it is born, does he not?

FREUD: Yes, but that is not for the baby's sake, but for the sake of more of the process. We get little enjoyment out of mere contemplation of the truth. We get much more out of the process of finding more truths. It is like gambling: it is the process of winning, not the winnings won, that excites us.

SOCRATES: There is something to what you say, I think.

FREUD: And that is why the first rule of the scientific method is to doubt everything, and always to keep an open mind. Which, by the way, is my critique of religion: it lacks that openness.

SOCRATES: But surely both science and religion seek truth, the one about nature and the other about the supernatural.

FREUD: Yes, but the door of the mind must always be kept open, if truth is your friend and you want to invite him in. Religion commands the mind to close, not to open.

SOCRATES: But what would a friend say if after he entered you kept the door open, so that he could also leave? Would that not be an insult? As a man named Chesterton once said, an open mind is like an open mouth: it is useful only for the purpose of clamping shut on something solid to eat.

FREUD: Clever but wrong, I think. And you surely know, Socrates, that arguments from analogies are perilous if not fallacious.

SOCRATES: So according to you, science does not really care as much as it pretends to care about knowing the truth?

FREUD: Again I must correct your logic, Socrates. "Science" is not a person. Do *people* care more about pleasure than about knowledge? Yes, they do.

SOCRATES: So that is why you make that surprising statement that science gives us a loosening of the connection with reality rather than a tightening of the connection.

FREUD: Yes. And even if this is not true of science, it is certainly true of art. Art does not reveal the real world but creates another world instead.

SOCRATES: So its end is also not truth but pleasure.

FREUD: Of course.

SOCRATES: But I think that this is contradicted by the data.

FREUD: What data?

SOCRATES: Why, the data of nearly all the greatest artists in the history of the world! For according to them, art also seeks to reveal truth, though a different kind of truth than science and in a different, non-literal way.

FREUD: Even if that were the purpose of *art*, I am talking about the motives of the *artist*, not the impersonal enterprise itself. Enterprises do not have motives, people do. I think you are confusing people with enterprises.

SOCRATES: And I think *you* are confusing subjective *motives* with objective *purposes* or ends. Enterprises *do* have purposes, though they don't have motives. That is why you can label contraception an unnatural perversion, as the whole human race did until after your time: because the personal motive contradicts the objective end or purpose.

FREUD: How does this mean I am wrong about art?

SOCRATES: It means you are wrong about the artist, about his motives. Great artists themselves almost always say that their motives are to reveal some truth.

FREUD: And I say that we seldom see what our real motives are. That is why psychology is a science: it tells us much more about ourselves than we thought we knew.

SOCRATES: Because our motives are usually subconscious rather than conscious?

FREUD: Yes.

SOCRATES: So our *real* motive in both art and science

is the same as our motive for using anaesthetics. It's "the pleasure principle" again.

FREUD: Yes.

SOCRATES: I wonder how you can justify calling one kind of motive more "real" than another just because it is subconscious rather than conscious. But I will not pursue that question, for it is part of the technical apparatus of your psychology, and I am investigating the *philosophical* implications of your book.

That is why what concerns me most in what you say here about art and science is your cruel dilemma: the closer to reality, the closer to misery; and correlatively, the closer to happiness, the farther from reality.

FREUD: It is sad but true. That is "the reality principle" versus "the pleasure principle."

SOCRATES: So the purpose of art is diversion from pain by pleasant illusions.

FREUD: Yes. I say that in art, **satisfaction is obtained from illusions, which are recognized as such without the discrepancy between them and reality being allowed to interfere with enjoyment.** I see you shaking your head. Why do you disagree with that?

SOCRATES: Because I believe in the data, and in the principle of believing in the data.

FREUD: Data? What data?

SOCRATES: People. People are data, aren't they?

FREUD: Of course.

SOCRATES: And people who experience a thing—no matter what it is: art, science, religion, psychoanalysis, philosophy, even headaches—mustn't these people know that thing better than the people who don't experience it? For they have data from experience that the others do not have, just as Galileo had data through his telescope that the bishops who refused to look through his telescope did not have.

FREUD: I believe that principle too. It is essential to all empirical science.

SOCRATES: Well, then, are you an artist?

FREUD: No.

SOCRATES: And *you* say that art is illusion. But the artists themselves almost never say that. They all claim to *reveal* something—something that *is* in some way, something real, though not empirically real, something true, though not literally true.

And sometimes what they want to reveal is painful, especially in modern art: for instance Giacometti, or Picasso.

So I would agree with you that art fails to solve the problem of "civilization and its discontents," but I would say that that is because its end is not to make us content but also to make us discontent. It seeks to afflict the comfortable as well as comfort the afflicted.

FREUD: How can the same thing have these two opposite ends?

SOCRATES: Only because neither of these two things is its ultimate end. Both contentment and discontentment can reveal reality, and *that* is the ultimate end of art, as also of science.

FREUD: So *you* say, Socrates, because you are a speculative philosopher.

SOCRATES: No, so say all the great artists and scientists.

FREUD: Just because they say it, that doesn't mean it's true.

SOCRATES: No, but is their view not more likely to be true than the view of an outsider?

FREUD: No! Not if they are idealizing their art, and exaggerating its importance. Isn't it more likely that they believe *too much* about art rather than that others believe too little?—that art, like religion, is deceptive precisely because it is so attractive and comforting?

SOCRATES: That is possible, yes. But that is also very cynical.

FREUD: That does not mean it is untrue.

SOCRATES: No. But it means that your world is very small.

FREUD: Or that yours is too large, because you think these artifices created by art and religion are objectively real. Tell me, Socrates, do you believe myths and fairy tales are true?

SOCRATES: I do indeed. Often a myth or a fairy tale can be truer than a statistic, even though its truth is not literal, scientific truth. There are other kinds, you know. Or, perhaps you don't. Surely "The Emperor's New Clothes" tells more truth about humanity than statistics about kings and robes and weavers in Denmark.

FREUD: But art arises from the creative imagination, not from the external world. And art is appreciated by the imagination, not by the senses or the reason. As I say, **The region from which these illusions arise is the life of the imagination. . . . At the head of these satisfactions through phantasy stands the enjoyment of works of art—an enjoyment which, by the agency of the artist, is made accessible even to those who are not themselves creative.**

And that is why the enjoyment of art is universal, though the ability to create it is not. See? I am not a snob or an elitist but an egalitarian.

SOCRATES: So you believe that only the senses and the reason can reveal truth, not the imagination?

FREUD: Yes.

SOCRATES: Then you *are* an elitist. For your evaluation of both art and imagination is very different from that of ordinary people. You say: **People who are receptive to the influence of art cannot set too high a value on it as a source of pleasure and consolation in life.** These "people who are receptive" apparently do not include yourself. So you are like the bishops, not like Galileo.

FREUD: I am not insensitive to the pleasures of art, Socrates. I too find pleasure and consolation in it.

SOCRATES: Do you think that "consolation" is the word most people would use to explain their love of art? Is it the word any great artist would use to explain his creation of it?

FREUD: Once again, Socrates, let me remind you that I am exploring the subconscious motives, not the conscious ones.

SOCRATES: That is your reason, your premise, your justification for your elitism. But your conclusion, your "bottom line," is still elitist. You still deeply disagree with the people who know and love the subject more than you do; and I think that is snobbery, no matter what your reason for it is.

Here is an even more telling instance of how different your understanding of art is than that of ordinary people. In noting how ineffective it is in making us content instead of discontent (which is quite true), you say: **Nevertheless the mild narcosis induced in us by art can do no more than bring about a transient withdrawal from the pressure of vital needs, and it is not strong enough to make us forget real misery.**

A "mild narcosis"—what a description of art! Art is for you only an inefficient drug!

FREUD: Is this your "logical" refutation of what I have said?

SOCRATES: No. In fact, I commend you on your logical consistency. For if, as you say, chemical intoxication is "the most effective means" to the end that you consider the closest anyone can get to happiness, namely the relief of suffering, then this—chemicals, drugs—must indeed be your touchstone, your standard for ranking everything else, all of which is then reduced to a less efficient narcotic.

FREUD: And your refutation of this is . . . ?

SOCRATES: Refutation? Did I say anything about refutation? Why would I even think of refutation? Isn't what you say irrefutable and obvious? Have not all the sages of all the ages said exactly the same thing? Has not the drug dealer always been regarded as the highest sage? Isn't it obvious that Shakespeare, Beethoven, Rembrandt, and Michelangelo, as well as their millions of lesser apprentices, would totally agree with you, and admit that the only reason they created their masterpieces was that adequate anaesthetics were not available in their day?

FREUD: You are "on a roll" now, Socrates. Just keep heaping it up; you don't need me to respond.

SOCRATES: So you have solved one of the great mysteries of philosophy, namely: What is the source of art? It is neither divine inspiration nor human creativity, it is the lack of intoxicants.

FREUD: I did not say that.

SOCRATES: No, no, wait, it makes sense. There is some evidence for it. For it is true that intoxicated people never produce great art. They do not need the mild intoxicant when they have the strong one. What a pity they cannot remain intoxicated forever! Then alone would they be content.

FREUD: I did not say that either.

SOCRATES: But you did imply that if only we had stronger and better narcotics, we would not need or prize the "mild narcosis" we get from Dante or Goethe or Mozart. For you say that the reason why the enjoyment of such works does not solve life's greatest problem is that it lacks the **"sating of crude and primary instinctual impulses; it does not convulse our physical being."**

FREUD: Since when did you abandon logic for sarcasm, Socrates?

SOCRATES: I did not abandon logic. In fact, I would like to explore a logical corollary of your view. Let us take any one art in particular, say music. Within this art, as within art in general, if you followed your "touchstone" principle about convulsions, judging everything as a kind of substitute for orgasm, you would logically have to rank as the very highest form of music "gangsta rap" or perhaps "heavy metal"; and you would have to rank as the very lowest something like Gregorian chant or Bach fugues, since your judgment is based on how many physical convulsions the art is able to produce, how close to orgasm it can get.

FREUD: I do not say that either.

SOCRATES: No, because you are less logical than I. And you are illogical because of fear: the fear of being refuted by my sarcastic "reductio ad absurdum." For fear is stronger than logic, after all, if you are right.

But it is time for a look at your fifth candidate.

11.
Insanity—and religion

SOCRATES: You write next,

Another procedure operates more energetically and more thoroughly. It regards reality as the sole enemy and as the source of all suffering, with which it is impossible to live, so that one must break off all relations with it if one is to be in any way happy. The hermit turns his back on the world and will have no truck with it. But one can do more than that; one can try to re-create the world, to build up in its stead another world in which its most unbearable features are eliminated and replaced by others that are in conformity with one's own wishes.

This is a logical progression from the last few candidates, each of which increases the amount of withdrawal from the real world, correct?

FREUD: Correct.

SOCRATES: And this one amounts to insanity.

FREUD: Yes.

SOCRATES: For the simplest touchstone of insanity is the refusal to live in the real world, the denial of the reality principle, the inability to distinguish between the real world and the dreamed-of world, which for you as a materialist means the distinction between the physical and the spiritual world. Would you agree with that?

FREUD: Yes. There *is* a non-physical, mental world but it is subjective, not objective.

SOCRATES: So this "solution" of insanity would be the most uncompromising insistence on the "pleasure principle" at the total expense of the reality principle.

FREUD: Yes. And that's why it simply cannot work, as I say next: **But whoever, in desperate defiance, sets out upon this path to happiness will as a rule attain nothing. Reality is too strong for him. He becomes a madman.**

SOCRATES: And you classify religion as an example of this.

FREUD: Yes.

SOCRATES: But if those who embrace religion "attain nothing," why do they embrace it? Why does it work for them?

FREUD: It doesn't.

SOCRATES: Oh, but it does, even by your standards. For instance, it holds off death a little longer. It make them live longer.

FREUD: Does it, really?

SOCRATES: Yes, really. You may check out the actuarial statistics on this. They are quite remarkable. The profession that lives longest is clergy. And there is a definite correlation between longevity and observable religious practices, like frequency of church attendance, time spent in prayer, and proportion of income given away in charity. The more religious you are, the longer you tend to live. Contemplative monks, who sacrifice the whole world for religion, live longer than anyone else.

FREUD: This is literally, scientifically, true?

SOCRATES: Yes. So I ask you: Do the insane live longer than the sane?

FREUD: No.

SOCRATES: But religious people live longer than the irreligious. So how can the religious be the insane? If insanity *shortens* both life and happiness, and religion *lengthens* both, how can religion be a form of insanity?

Religious believers also show fewer of the obvious marks of unhappiness: suicide, violence, depression, stress. If insanity makes us unhappy and religions makes us happy, how can religion be insanity?

FREUD: There are species of insanity that put a smile on our face. These super-religious people may be like some of the people in insane asylums: they may feel happier, but are they, really?

SOCRATES: I am surprised to hear that distinction from you, Sigmund: the distinction between objectively true happiness and subjectively felt contentment. I wonder why you waited until now to use it. I quite agree that feelings are no index of truth.

But I wonder why religion makes these people at least *feel* happier? And why does it make them live longer? Those effects are certainly not "nothing."

FREUD: But they do not prove it to be true rather than illusory.

SOCRATES: That is quite correct, and quite reasonable and in accord with common sense. But you shock even the common sense of non-religious people or agnostics like myself when you say that **The religions of mankind must be classified among the mass-delusions of this kind.** So you believe that religion is literally insanity.

FREUD: I suspected you would not agree with my reasoning here, Socrates.

SOCRATES: On the contrary, I commend you for being much more logically consistent than most people are. For if religion is not true, then the only thing it could possibly be would be the greatest of all illusions, the most unrealistic of all dreams, in fact the greatest of all insanities.

FREUD: I think know where you are going with this, Socrates. It is a left-handed compliment. After commending me for my logical consistency, you will say that my entire argument is another "reductio ad absurdum." You will argue that if religion is false, it is insanity; and it is absurd to call all religion insanity; therefore I am wrong to say religion is false.

SOCRATES: That is not what I was going to say at all. Perhaps I will eventually come to the conclusion that your argument is indeed a "reductio ad absurdum" and that atheism is false, but I do not know that yet. As an agnostic about the nature of the God or gods, I do not claim to know that your atheism is simply absurd, or even that it is false. But it does seem absurd to call all religion not just false but literally insanity.

FREUD: Yet the logic is compelling. If it is not true, it is like believing in the invisible playmate you imagined when you were two, even when you are grown up. And the fact that billions of others believe it does not make it any more true or any less insane.

SOCRATES: Your logical consistency is admirable, Sigmund. But it is a two-edged sword: it may just as well turn one *to* religion as against it. For if religion *is* true, then it is atheism that is the insanity. It is like not recognizing your parents' existence even though they gave you life and continue to give you love and food and gifts.

And there is still the problem of snobbery, which you atheists have but the religious believers do not have. To be an atheist you have to believe that the mass of mankind are literally insane, and that you few atheists are, not merely the only ones who are correct, or even the only ones who are wise, but the only ones who are *sane*.

FREUD: But you admit, then, that one of these two groups—either the believers or the atheists—must be insane.

SOCRATES: The logic seems to necessitate that conclusion, yes.

FREUD: I am surprised to hear you admit that, Socrates. I thought you would say that we cannot know whether religion is true or not, and that therefore agnosticism is the reasonable position, and that meanwhile we should respect piety and follow the highest values, which are those values that all the religions of the world preach, even if we do not know whether they are true or not.

SOCRATES: No, I do not say that. Logic compels me to agree with you here. If religion is not true, it is not worth following because it is literally insanity. As you say, it is then like an adult still believing in the literal existence of the invisible friend he invented when he was a very small child, and adoring this invisible imaginary person as the most important person in the world and the center of his life, seeking his advice in everything, conforming to his imagined will in everything, loving him and investing all his hopes of happiness in him. For instance, let's say this invisible friend is a very large and benign invisible rabbit named "Harvey." Such a person we would rightly regard as literally insane, I think, if and only if one condition obtained.

FREUD: What?

SOCRATES: That Harvey is not real, of course.

FREUD: Of course.

SOCRATES: But what if he *was* real?

FREUD: How could an imaginary rabbit be real?

SOCRATES: He couldn't. But suppose he is not imaginary. Suppose he *is* real. In that case, those who do *not* believe in him would be the ones who are not living in the real world, would they not? And is that not the definition of insanity?

FREUD: Are you seriously proposing this possibility? That I and all my fellow atheists are literally insane?

SOCRATES: I follow the argument wherever it leads, and the logic seems to lead to that conclusion. Once again, consider the consequences if the majority is right and God or gods exist. Would not atheists then be like children who live in their parents' house without acknowledging the existence of the parents, who eat the parents' food and accept the parents' gifts without ever looking at them or speaking to them or thanking them or even paying the slightest attention to them, but believe that the existence of parents is a great illusion—would not such children be literally insane?

FREUD: I suppose you could say that.

SOCRATES: So it may be that it is not the children who speak to this invisible friend who are insane, but the children who do *not* speak to Him.

FREUD: But everyone knows that childhood invisible friends are unreal.

SOCRATES: Oh, so now you are accepting "what everyone knows"—the authority of the vast majority? Why then do you not apply this principle when it comes to religion?

FREUD: Because the two cases are very different. And the difference is not just a matter of numbers. The parents are visible. The invisible friend is not.

SOCRATES: So your assumption is that only the visible is real.

FREUD: Yes.

SOCRATES: That assumption is also not believed by the vast majority. And it is an assumption. It cannot be proved. It has never been proved. It is a faith, an ideology, a kind of religion.

FREUD: Irreligion is a religion? Is that what you call logic?

SOCRATES: It is a *faith*, at least.

FREUD: But the evidence is all in favor of this faith and not the other.

SOCRATES: What evidence?

FREUD: The success of science, for one thing.

SOCRATES: But does not the success of science depend on the order and design of the world? And of the fit between our minds and the world? And does not religion have an explanation for that fit in the notion that an intelligent God designed and created both our minds and the world? So the success of science would seem to count *for* religion rather than against it.

Unless, of course, some particular discovery of some particular science has clearly disproved some particular dogma of religion. But if that had ever happened, no educated and intelligent and honest person could believe that religion any more, because it would then not be a matter of faith but a matter of proof. Has any such proof of the falsehood of religion ever been found by science? Have the bones of the dead Jesus been found in Palestine and identified by DNA testing?

FREUD: There is no data to disprove the invisible rabbit. There is no scientific proof or disproof of religion. That's why I offer psychological evidence rather than physical evidence. And my psychology explains religion. It may not *prove* atheism, but it makes it *probable*. But there are no good arguments that make religion even probable.

SOCRATES: I thought we just found one. We both admitted that if religion is untrue, believers are insane, and that if atheism is untrue, then atheists are insane, did we not?

FREUD: Yes.

SOCRATES: And since atheists make up perhaps five per cent of people, it logically follows that either five or ninety five percent of people are insane, does it not?

FREUD: Yes.

SOCRATES: Now which is more probable? Is it not more likely, at least, that it is the small minority rather than the vast majority who are insane?

FREUD: How could that be calculated? There are no good analogies.

SOCRATES: Of course there is: a very obvious one.

FREUD: What?

SOCRATES: Insanity for all other reasons, of course.

FREUD: How would you calculate probabilities, then? I don't understand.

SOCRATES: We label people insane when we think they simply are not living in the real world any more, don't we?

FREUD: Yes.

SOCRATES: And therefore we put them in asylums and try to heal them, or at least protect the rest of the world from them by isolating them.

FREUD: Yes. So what?

SOCRATES: Well, I ask you: Which of these two situations is the more likely? Is it that the world is populated by a large number of sane people—foolish and wicked, perhaps, but not literally insane—who surround the few insane people that they have accurately labeled insane and put into asylums? Or that almost the entire surrounding world is insane and that those few whom the rest of the world has labeled insane and put into asylums are in fact the only sane ones? Do you think the second view is more probable?

FREUD: I see how threatening that view would be, but I do not see how that makes it impossible.

SOCRATES: It also makes it incredibly arrogant and snobbish: that we few alone are the sane.

FREUD: But that does not prove it is not *true,* just psychologically threatening.

SOCRATES: I would call it more than "threatening."

FREUD: What would you call it?

SOCRATES: To use a psychological term, I would call it paranoia.

FREUD: Why?

SOCRATES: Would you not call it paranoia to believe that nineteen out of twenty people you meet every day—your family, your friends, your partners at work—are literally insane?

FREUD: I suppose so.

SOCRATES: But that is what you have to believe if atheism is true, by your own admission, if religion is insanity.

FREUD: Perhaps I exaggerated in calling religion insanity. The consequences seem rather severe.

SOCRATES: Our old "reductio ad absurdum" looks threatening once again, doesn't it?

FREUD: But I am not finished. I have another critique of religion, which is based on observation and not based on any kind of faith.

SOCRATES: I am happy to hear it.

FREUD: Perhaps it is as you say: perhaps the question of whether religion is insanity or not does depend on whether there is a God or not. But the existence of God is unverifiable by experience and scientific reasoning, and there is something else that is quite verifiable by experience, and that is my critique of religion from the standpoint of empirical psychology—and this critique has no assumptions, no kind of "faith," as you put it. This critique comes in the last paragraph of this chapter, where I make the following point, if you will allow me to quote my own book.

SOCRATES: Of course. Go ahead.

FREUD: I observe that **The man who is predominantly erotic will give first preference to his emotional relationships to other people; the narcissistic man, who inclines to be self-sufficient, will seek his main satisfactions in his internal mental processes; the man of action will never give up the external world on which he can try out his strength. (And) the man who sees his pursuit of happiness come to nothing in later years can still find consolation in the yield of pleasure of chronic intoxication.** This division of human types was evident even to Aristotle. But **Religion restricts this play of choice and adaption, since it imposes equally on everyone its own path to the acquisition of happiness and protection**

from suffering. Its technique consists in depressing the value of life and distorting the picture of the real world in a delusional manner—which presupposes an intimidation of the intelligence.

SOCRATES: This is indeed a common critique of religion. I am not a religious apologist—I am indeed an agnostic, as you said—but from a logical point of view I find some very questionable things in this passage.

FREUD: Why does that not surprise me?

SOCRATES: The answer to that question is either because you are humble enough to expect to commit some errors, or because you are arrogant enough to assume that I will find some even though they do not exist. But in either case, here are my objections. There are quite a few of them.

The first concerns your characterization of the first kind of person, who seeks happiness in his relationships to other people. This person need not be "emotional." The saints all found their meaning in loving others, but their relationship was not an emotional one. The love they pursued was not *eros* but *agape*. What moved them was the will to the other person's good, not the desire for their own emotional satisfaction. Your cynicism seems to blind you to the data.

Second, even more questionable is your confinement of this unselfish love to persons whom you call "predominantly erotic." That is at least a very questionable interpretation of Jesus and the saints. It seems to assume that all relationships are sexual. I know that is your position, but I do not see that you have proved it, and it certainly does not *seem* to be the case. Again, you seem to deny the data.

Third, you reduce the second kind of person, whom you call self-sufficient, to "the narcissistic man." Apparently you have thinkers like myself in mind—and yourself as well, perhaps. Are we both concerned with embracing our reflection in the water, like Narcissus, rather than discovering objective truth in our different fields? Is that a fair characterization of either one of us?

Fourth, you say that religion "imposes equally on everyone its own path." But does not science do the same? Does not every objective truth do this? So your critique *presupposes* that religion is not a matter of objective truth. For if it were, it would no more "impose its path" than science does, or ordinary everyday sense perception does

Fifth, calling religion a "distortion" and "an intimidation of the intelligence" is rhetoric, not argument—and, in fact, is precisely an example of what it accuses religion of, namely an intimidation of the intelligence. The religious person could equally call your atheism a "distortion" and "an intimidation of the intelligence." The alternative to intimidation is argument, not words that blame rather than describe; especially words that beg the question.

Finally, you say religion "consists in depressing the value of life." I suppose you mean that all religion says that the world that appears to our senses is not the highest world, but that there is a higher and better and truer one; thus this world is ranked second rather than first. Is that what you meant?

FREUD: Yes.

SOCRATES: But this lowering of the world's value is relative, not absolute. To say that 10 is less than 20 is not to say it is less than 10. If you had 10 gold pieces and no one else had any more than 10, you would be the richest. But if someone had 20, you would still be just as rich. It is only envy that might make you feel poor. So could it possibly be envy of God that makes you prefer to think of yourself as one whose first cause and ultimate end lie in this world rather than in a higher one? Is that why you think of yourself as the child of King Kong rather than the child of King God?

FREUD: Clever rhetoric, Socrates, but facts are facts. Religion depresses the value of life.

SOCRATES: Let's get specific. Which religion did you have in mind here?

FREUD: All of them.

SOCRATES: But I suppose you mean especially the two religions you knew the best and which were the most influential in Western civilization, namely Judaism and Christianity.

FREUD: Yes.

SOCRATES: I wonder how these two religions "depress the value of life," since they claim that life takes place in a world created by God and declared "good" after each day's work of creation, culminating in God declaring man "very good."

FREUD: Well, Judaism sometimes affirms life, but Christianity is horribly ascetic.

SOCRATES: But Christianity puts an even higher value on human life, especially on the human body, because its central doctrine is that God Himself took on human life and a human body, and saved mankind from sin and death and Hell by the gift of His body. What could possibly put a higher value on life and the body than that?

FREUD: But what about those ascetics?

SOCRATES: They are a strange and small minority. Should we judge the effect of a religion on a civilization by exceptional cases or by normal ones?

FREUD: Even normal people are repressed by religion.

SOCRATES: Why are they "repressed" if religion gives them positive things to do that make them happier, like faith and hope and love?

FREUD: They are told how to behave. They are told that only if they obey the "straight and narrow way" can they be happy, and if they disobey it, they will be miserable.

SOCRATES: And what is wrong with that, if it is true?

FREUD: It isn't true.

SOCRATES: Then why are they so happy?

And why are you so miserable?

And why do you have no answer to those questions?

12.
What's Wrong with Love?

SOCRATES: But we should return to your investigation of other paths to happiness. Next comes the most interesting option of all, and one with many surprises.

FREUD: Love, you mean.

SOCRATES: Yes.

FREUD: What are the surprises?

SOCRATES: First, that you rank it so low. Second, that you never even think of classifying it under religion, or even connecting these two things, love and religion, even though you consider love immediately after you consider religion (which you classify as insanity).

FREUD: Oh, but I do connect them. I explain, just a little later, how religion sublimates love and tries to change it into something spiritual and unselfish.

SOCRATES: But have you ever considered the opposite possibility?

FREUD: What is that?

SOCRATES: That it is you who sublimate spiritual love and change it into something physical and selfish. I see by your look of utter surprise that you never have considered that.

But we will get to what you say about sublimation in a few minutes. Here is how you begin your consideration of love:

I do not think that I have made a complete enumeration of the methods by which men strive to gain happiness and keep suffering away, and I know, too, that the material might have been differently arranged. One procedure I have not yet mentioned—not because I have forgotten it but because it will concern us later in another connection . . . I am, of course, speaking of the way of life which makes love the centre of everything, which looks for all satisfaction in loving and being loved. A psychical attitude of this sort comes naturally enough to all of us; (for) one of the forms in which love manifests itself—sexual love—has given us our most intense experience of an overwhelming sensation of pleasure and has thus furnished us with a pattern for our search for happiness. What is more natural than that we should persist in looking for happiness along the path on which we first encountered it?

Once again we find you taking orgasm as your archetype, your touchstone, your absolute. I suppose I should not find *that* surprising. But I do I find it rather surprising that the form of love which you say "comes naturally enough to all of us" is a love we encounter only later in life, not the very first form of love that we encounter, long before puberty, namely the love of parents, and the trust in their love and protection and wisdom.

Isn't this the form of love that we would most likely project into the cosmos in the form of a God? Wouldn't this form of love more naturally lead to religion? You yourself seem to imply this when you say that religion originates in the need for a cosmic father.

FREUD: That is a reasonable explanation. What do you find "surprising" in what I say?

SOCRATES: That you do not use it. That you do not explain both religion and the later, erotic love by the simpler and earlier childlike form of love. That would be an evolutionary explanation, reducing the complex to the simple and the later to the earlier, which is a basic principle of your method in every other case. Why did you not use it here?

FREUD: I don't know. Why do *you* think? Psychoanalyze me, Socrates.

SOCRATES: Oh, that's too easy, Sigmund. It's like pointing out the sun on a clear summer day. Isn't it obvious? Your obsession with sexual pleasure seems to overwhelm your logical consistency here. And your lack of experience or understanding of actual children too, for you even imply, in the last sentence I quoted, that children cannot be happy.

FREUD: How do I imply that?

SOCRATES: You say: **What is more natural than that we should persist in looking for happiness along the path on which we first encountered it.**

FREUD: How does that mean that children cannot be happy?

SOCRATES: You here call *sexual* love our *first* encounter with happiness.

FREUD: I do.

SOCRATES: Well, that implies that our encounters with the other, pre-pubescent forms of love were *not* encounters with happiness.

FREUD: I suppose you think you have psychoanalyzed me now?

SOCRATES: No, my work is to find unconscious premises, not motives. Psychoanalysis is no more my competence than logical analysis is yours.

FREUD: We are equal, then.

SOCRATES: Except that I know and admit my ignorance and incompetence, while you do not.

FREUD: But if Plato reported your views accurately in his "Symposium," you championed love, and said it was the only thing you claimed certain knowledge about.

SOCRATES: Even if that was what I actually said, and not Plato's invention, I am not evaluating your philosophy by the standard of my philosophy, but only by the standard of logical consistency and the data of experience.

So let us examine your reason for rejecting love as the answer to the question of life's greatest value. You say:

The weak side of this technique of living is easy to see; otherwise no human being would have thought of abandoning this path to happiness for any other. It is that we are never so defenseless against suffering as when we love, never so helplessly unhappy as when we have lost our loved object or its love.

FREUD: So what is your critique of my critique of love?

SOCRATES: My first reaction is to praise you for your insight. It is true, indeed, and part of the data of common human experience, that **we are never so defenseless against suffering as when we love.** Love multiplies our sufferings by the two factors of the number of people we love and the depth with which we love them. For to love is to identify one's self and one's good and one's happiness with the other.

FREUD: I sense a very big "but" coming.

SOCRATES: You are correct. If you will compare our respective anatomies, you will find that my butt is much bigger than yours.

FREUD: I can see your butt, but what is your "but"?

SOCRATES: It is that you forget that love also multiples our *joys* by the very same two factors.

FREUD: But . . .

SOCRATES: I think perhaps your "but" is going to prove bigger than mine here.

FREUD: But the sufferings cut deeper than the joys.

SOCRATES: That is, indeed, your presupposition throughout your work. And I accept that as true—for you. That is your feeling, and feelings are indeed subjective truths, if we can call them truths at all. But this is *not* true for the majority of mankind, who willingly accept the bitter with the sweet, the sorrows with the joys, in choosing to love. If you are right in saying that all men seek happiness, then it must be that these people—who are the majority—judge that a life of love contains greater joys than sorrows, that the joys are wroth the sorrows. Otherwise they would not invest their psychic energy in an enterprise doomed to failure and bankruptcy, unless they were so stupid that they think their loves will be utterly unlike all the other loves they see around them in this vale of tears, and be free from pain and suffering.

But that is not my sharpest criticism of this passage. I am far more shocked by your pronoun.

FREUD: My pronoun?

SOCRATES: You first speak of **our loved object or *its* love.** First you speak of the "loved *object*" rather than the loved *person*, then you refer to this person as an **it** rather than as a **she.**

FREUD: I thus avoided male chauvinism, of which I am often accused.

SOCRATES: But you did this only by sacrificing human-chauvinism. You avoided reducing women to men by reducing both to things! I can think of no greater insult. To be called a stupid man, or a wicked man, or a foolish man, or a weak man, or an ugly man, or an unmanly man—these are all far less insulting than to be called a thing, an *it.* That becomes true only at death, when you become a corpse. Only then does *I* become *it.* So this pronoun amounts to mental murder.

FREUD: It was a slip of the pen, Socrates. You are exaggerating a grammatical error.

SOCRATES: I think not, for two reasons. First, because your most famous psychological doctrine, about the id, ego and superego, claims that the true self is not the ego, the I, but the id, which literally means "it." It is you who chose those pronouns, deliberately. And second, in the later section of the book, which you refer to here, and where you say more about love, you continue to deliberately use the word "love-object" and the pronoun "it."

In this passage you identify sexual love with genital love. Was *that* a slip of the pen?

FREUD: No.

SOCRATES: Then I think your reduction of sexual love to genital love is as questionable as your reduction of all love to sexual love. Even most of your fellow psychologists and most of your fellow atheists would not agree with you there, I think. And this reductionism is another insult to the person and the personal, for it implies that a lover's adoring contemplation of his beloved's uniquely personal face is really nothing but a longing for genital intercourse with the more impersonal and common parts of her body.

FREUD: Do you want to go into my reasons for classifying all love as genital?

SOCRATES: To be honest, no.

But I do want to explore the later passage that you call **a digression which will enable us to fill in a gap which we left in an earlier discussion . . . We said there that man's discovery that sexual (genital) love afforded him the prototype of all happiness, must have suggested to him that he should continue to seek the satisfaction of happiness in his life along the path of sexual relations and that he should make genital eroticism the central point of his life. We went on to say that in doing so he made himself dependent in a most dangerous way on a portion of the external world, namely, his chosen love-object, and exposed himself to extreme suffering if he should be rejected by that object or should lose it through unfaithfulness or death.**

There you go again with all those flattering, romantic names for Juliet: "a portion of the external world," not another subject but a "love-*object*," an "it."

And then you say something that is literally

astonishing: **For that reason the wise men of every age have warned us most emphatically against this way of life.** What I find astonishing is those first three words: "For that reason." With those three words you say that all the great teachers of the past who disagreed with your making "genital eroticism the central point of life," all the religious and nonreligious versions of "Thou shalt not commit adultery" in history, have had *this* as their reason for saying that genital eroticism was not the very greatest and most central thing in all of life; it was not any of the higher reasons or motives they *thought* they had. So when Buddha, or his Hindu predecessors, or Moses, or Jesus, or Muhammad said that selfish lust is not as high or holy or happy as unselfish altruism, their real reason was only the purely pragmatic problem of suffering.

Your ability to see the deepest motives of the greatest men you have never met better than they see themselves is truly Godlike, Sigmund. In fact, I am amazed that you are still an atheist when you believe in such godlike powers as those.

FREUD: To arguments, I can respond with other arguments; but to sarcastic insults, I cannot.

SOCRATES: Do you really believe that if some miraculous or technological discovery had overcome the problem of the "love-object's" unfaithfulness or death, all these teachers would have told the world, "Go copulate at will, like the animals."?

FREUD: No indeed. No culture ever has said this, or ever can. In fact the central problem of the second half of my book is the paradox that civilization *must* restrict sexual activity, and thus thwart sexual pleasure, so that the very thing we have invented to expand our happiness—civilization—must always contract it. And that is not dependent on any religious or moral systems or beliefs, but is inherent in the human situation.

SOCRATES: But you insist that no higher motives are involved? Your psychoanalysis of Jesus, Buddha, Moses and the rest still stands?

FREUD: I do not say those were their *conscious* motives. The conscious mind seldom knows its own underlying, operative motives, Socrates.

SOCRATES: But you say those were their subconscious motives. And since the subconscious motives are the operative ones, the most real ones, those were their real motives.

FREUD: Yes. But you needn't make sarcastic jokes about my divinity.

SOCRATES: I can't help it. Because I can't help being in awe at how much wiser you are in understanding all these sages than they were in understanding themselves.

FREUD: I am not the arrogant idiot you imply I am, Socrates. For I do not claim certainty, only probability. In fact, my method has been called a "hermeneutic of *suspicion.*"

SOCRATES: Since you do not claim divinity or exemption from the human condition, the same "suspicion" must attach to your own work.

FREUD: Of course!

SOCRATES: Including that judgment itself. It too, like the judgments of the sages, must have been motivated not by an honest search for truth for its own sake, but by the frustrations of your personal desire for "genital eroticism." For if you are right, then *everything* is, deep down, moved by this force, like a First Mover—like a God, almost.

FREUD: I do not exempt myself from that conclusion. But there are no gods here.

SOCRATES: In that case, as I asked you before, why should I believe what you say? If all human reasoning is really only the rationalizing of our sexual eroticism, then the reasoning that produced that judgment can be no different. So your "hermeneutic of suspicion" really cancels out its own authority, or destroys its own credentials. It saws off the branch it sits on. It commits intellectual suicide. Your method is self-contradictory. That is the most fundamental of all logical fallacies: self-contradiction.

FREUD: And *that* is an excellent example of passive-aggressive behavior, Socrates: pretending to be the logical, objective, fair and honest philosopher who has no hidden personal motives, as the rest of us have. I think it is you, not I, who are claiming a divine prerogative.

SOCRATES: And *that* is another famous fallacy, the "ad hominem": attacking the arguer instead of the argument. It is also the "genetic fallacy," confusing the personal, motivational "because" with the logical "because."

FREUD: Are we here to trade insults or to examine texts?

SOCRATES: To examine texts. So let us continue to do what we are here to do.

You next write: **A small minority are enabled by their constitution to find happiness, in spite of everything, along the path of love.**

So you are saying that despite the fact that the vast majority of people believe that love is the path to the highest human happiness, it is really only "a small minority" who can accomplish this. So again you claim to know ordinary people far better than they know themselves.

FREUD: That's what they paid me for, Socrates!

SOCRATES: And you say that what enables this "small minority" to find happiness in love is not their moral character, or their religious faith, or their free choices, but "their constitution," their physical and chemical makeup, their biological heredity—something they are not personally responsible for. So then we should stop praising unselfish saints, and blaming selfish sinners. A convenient philosophy for tyrants!

FREUD: This from the man who said he was not here for insults!

SOCRATES: It is your philosophy, not yourself, that I am insulting, Sigmund.

FREUD: You are assuming the possibility of making that distinction, and of thus rising to the level of impersonal reason.

SOCRATES: I see your point, Sigmund. There is no such distinction if your philosophy is correct; if, as Nietzsche said, all systems of philosophy are no more than personal confessions.

FREUD: Quite so. It is natural that you would be

threatened by that insight. It would put you out of work. It would make *your* "thing" (philosophy) a fake rather than mine.

SOCRATES: I see we *are* back to the level of insult.

FREUD: And I see that you personally identify with your "thing" as much as I do with mine!

SOCRATES: But even if that is so, there is a difference: My "thing" is objective while yours is subjective. I disappear into my "thing," while your "thing" disappears into you.

FREUD: You do *not* disappear. No one does.

SOCRATES: Except the beloved, who disappears into an "it"?

FREUD: You are exalting my pronouns into a philosophy.

SOCRATES: But *you* are reducing *him*s and *her*s into *it*s, your friends and family into things.

FREUD: Whether I am "reducing" or you are "exalting," you are assuming that we can rise above this projecting and attain some "objective truth." But I am not assuming that.

SOCRATES: I think we have come to the heart of our disagreement, about "objective truth." And that means that we have made some significant progress, to have identified our central difference.

But I fear we will make no more progress if we stay here, with this point, for there are no common premises that we can both accept that would lead to conclusions that would make one of us right and the other wrong. You assume that objectivity, or impersonal reason, are not possible, and I assume that they are. And we differ even over whether that very question can be addressed objectively, impersonally, rationally, and honestly.

FREUD: So what shall we do?

SOCRATES: Let's become more specific. Let's see what we find when we return to what you have written about love.

FREUD: Perhaps this is why we have my book in our hands, as an anchor, to counter the drifts of the currents of our argument, so that we do not drift away endlessly into philosophical abstractions.

SOCRATES: Good. So here is how you explain altruistic love in your book:

You assume the same anthropology as Machiavelli and Hobbes do: you assume that we are all by nature simply selfish and materialistic, that unselfish love does not come from our nature, as selfish love does. You write:

A small minority are enabled by their constitution to find happiness, in spite of everything, along the path of love. But far-reaching mental changes in the function of love are necessary before this can happen. (1) These people make themselves independent of their object's acquiescence by displacing what they mainly value from being loved on to loving; (2) they protect themselves against the loss of the object by directing their love not to single objects but to all men alike; and (3) they avoid the uncertainties and disappointments of genital love by turning away from its sexual aims and transforming the instinct into an impulse with an *inhibited* aim. What they bring

about in themselves in this way is a state of evenly suspended, steadfast, affectionate feeling, which has little external resemblance any more to the stormy agitations of genital love, from which it is nevertheless derived. Perhaps St. Francis of Assisi went furthest in thus exploiting love for the benefit of an inner feeling of happiness.

I think this is an amazing distortion of unselfish love, and reveals only that you have never either experienced it or understood it, either in another or in yourself.

FREUD: Prove it. Prove that it is I who distort love, rather than the saints. Refute my "distortions."

SOCRATES: Fine. But there are so many distortions that it will take a long time.

First, unselfish lovers do *not* "make themselves independent of their object's acquiescence." The obvious example of this unselfish love is *motherhood*. Does a mother not care whether her children love her back or reject her love? Did Jesus not care whether his disciples reciprocated God's love or rejected it, whether they went to Heaven or to Hell?

Second, they do *not* "direct their love not to single objects but to all men alike." Do mothers love strangers' children as much as their own? Does a saint love only the abstraction "humanity"? Do they love all men the same even though they *are* not the same? Or do they love them as they are? Do they not love each individual as a unique individual?

Third, is this charity nothing but sexual inhibition? Is there no difference between a repressed Victorian and a saint?

Fourth, as far as the saints are concerned, you apparently know none of them except the only one your secular culture made famous, for reasons quite other than sanctity, St. Francis of Assisi. That is like claiming to understand psychology by knowing only Sigmund Freud. St. Francis was indeed a saint, but not the greatest one; and he did not "*go furthest* in exploiting love."

Fifth, is this the real motive for exercising charity?—not any real love of the other's good but only the selfish subconscious calculation that I must make myself independent of suffering? Are unselfish lovers fools who do not know themselves? Or are they deliberate fakes and liars about their motives? Must our suspicion be directed to the saints more than to the sinners?

Sixth, you describe charity or unselfish love as "a state of evenly suspended, steadfast, affectionate feeling." The *only* correct word in that whole description is "steadfast."

Charity is not "evenly suspended"; that is justice.

Nor is charity "affection"; that is another kind of love altogether. Affection is an instinct, shared by higher animals such as dogs and cats. It is not a free choice.

And charity is not a "feeling" but a choice of the will. If it were a feeling, it could not be commanded. If it is a feeling, then all the saints and moralists and religious teachers who commanded it were fools, who were really saying, "I command you to have spontaneous feelings of affection for all men, even lepers and liars and fools and Freudians."

FREUD: Another low blow, Socrates. You are a regular street brawler.

SOCRATES: Names will never hurt me.

FREUD: I do admit that charity is highly respected.

SOCRATES: Yes, you do say that **According to one**

ethical view (it is, in fact, not just "one ethical view" but the single commonest ethical imperative in the world, found in nearly every culture and summarized in what we call the "golden rule"), **whose deeper motivation will become clear to us presently** (oh, oh, another reductionism coming), **this readiness for a universal love of mankind and the world represents the highest standpoint which man can reach.**

But then you give us two astonishingly cynical objections to this universal ethic of charity: **Even at this early stage of the discussion I should like to bring forward my two main objections to this view. A love that does not discriminate seems to me to forfeit a part of its own value, by doing an injustice to its object; and secondly, not all men are worthy of love.**

But charity *does* discriminate. It discriminates between persons because it loves each individual as an individual, not as a cardboard cutout or copy. It is concrete, not abstract!

And it discriminates between good and evil in loving evil persons because of their *need* of goodness and good persons because of their *possession* of it.

It also discriminates between itself and justice by deliberately loving people not in proportion to their deservingness, as justice does, but in proportion to their need. And your critique of the love that deliberately goes beyond justice is—that it goes beyond justice!

Of course "not all men are worthy of love." That's the whole point of love: that it goes beyond worth, beyond dessert, beyond justice. Your second objection says nothing more than your first. You *blame* charity for going beyond justice. That's like blaming Aphrodite for being more beautiful than Xanthippe. You give no *reason* for ranking justice higher than charity. And you set yourself against nearly all human value systems here, against nearly all the great ethical teachers in human history.

FREUD: Such as Machiavelli, Hobbes, Hume, Mill, and Nietzsche?

SOCRATES: Perhaps I should have said "against all the *ethical* ethical teachers."

FREUD: I know who you mean. But I am not an idealist.

SOCRATES: I wonder. When you are in need of charity rather than justice—when you are in need of forgiveness, when you are "unworthy" because you are old and useless and ugly, or because you have done something wicked and unlovable—would you really prefer that the people around you treat you with justice unmixed with mercy or charity? Do you want justice rather than love from your family? Or do you, perhaps, consider yourself one of the few men who *are* "worthy of love"?

FREUD: My book is not a personal autobiography or a self-psychoanalysis. It is an impersonal, objective, scientific investigation. From that perspective, it is certainly true that "not all men are worthy of love." I am a realist.

SOCRATES: And so am I. In fact, that is precisely the reason charity is needed, and not just justice. In an ideal world justice would be sufficient, but the "realistic" fact that men are not worthy of love is precisely the reason that charity is so much more prized than justice.

FREUD: You cannot run a laboratory, a government, an

army, or a business on charity, Socrates. It must be run on justice.

SOCRATES: But even Aristotle, that supreme realist and master of common sense and empirical observation, noted that a city is held together more firmly and happily by friendship than by justice.

FREUD: I have no qualms against disagreeing with Aristotle!

SOCRATES: Let's see if you really do. Tell me, do you agree that justice and duty are correlative? That doing your duty means doing what is just?

FREUD: Yes.

SOCRATES: So that charity, in going beyond justice, goes beyond duty?

FREUD: Yes.

SOCRATES: How, then, do you evaluate the fact that most men praise actions that "go beyond the call of duty," like rushing into a burning building to save a stranger's baby?

FREUD: Socrates, I am not a moral monster; I admire such behavior as much as others do. My point is merely that a life founded and centered on such love is unrealistic.

SOCRATES: Why would you call it "unrealistic"? It is real. It exists. Many people do aspire to it as their supreme value. Most men try to live by it. Of course, no one lives it perfectly; but, then, no one lives *any* ideal perfectly, including justice and duty.

FREUD: It is unrealistic because it is an artifice, though

perhaps a noble artifice, like a delicate sculpture. It is a sublimation of something that is more real, something that is natural and innate and instinctual, namely biological love, sexual love. That is what I point out in my next paragraph. I say:

The love which founded the family continues to operate in civilization both in its original form, in which it does not renounce direct sexual satisfaction, and in its modified form as aim-inhibited affection . . . People give the name 'love' to the relation between a man and a woman whose genital needs have led them to found a family; but they also give the name 'love' to the positive feelings between parents and children, and between the brothers and sisters of a family, although *we* are obliged to describe this as 'aim-inhibited love' or 'affection.' Love with an inhibited aim was in fact originally fully sensual love, and it is so still in man's unconscious.

SOCRATES: If I am not misunderstanding you here, I find this another quite astonishing passage—as most readers would, I'm sure. You seem to be saying that even natural affection (*storge*) and charity (*agape*) and friendship (*philia)* are really erotic love (*eros*) in disguise, eros with a chastity belt, eros with its aim or natural end "inhibited," so that the love now aims not at the physical pleasures of genital intercourse but at something more spiritual and more altruistic, the good of the other. Am I misunderstanding you?

FREUD: No, that is exactly what I mean.

SOCRATES: So when a mother cuddles her baby, she really, deep down, in her unconscious, wants to have intercourse with the baby. And when a big brother defends his little sister against a bully, or when a father defends his family against a robber or a corporation, he is really only sublimating a desire for genital sex.

FREUD: Dark and surprising indeed are the mysteries of the unconscious, Socrates.

SOCRATES: And the seventh and last candidate for the "summum bonum," which you mention after the long section on love—namely, "the enjoyment of beauty"—this too you reduce to sex. You say:

We may go on from here to consider the interesting case in which happiness in life is predominantly sought in the enjoyment of beauty, wherever beauty presents itself to our senses and our judgment . . . This aesthetic attitude to the goal of life offers little protection against the threat of suffering, but it can compensate for a great deal. The enjoyment of beauty has a peculiar, mildly intoxicating quality of feeling. Beauty has no obvious use; nor is there any clear cultural necessity for it. Yet civilization could not do without it. The science of aesthetics investigates the conditions under which things are felt as beautiful, but it has been unable to give any explanation of the nature and origin of beauty . . . Psychoanalysis, unfortunately, has scarcely anything to say about beauty either. All that seems certain is its derivation from the field of sexual feeling. The love of beauty seems a perfect example of an impulse with an inhibited aim.

So the one thing you say is certain about beauty is this: that when the artist enjoys watching a sunset and wants to paint it, this is another "aim-inhibited love," and he really wants to have intercourse with it. But because it is too hot, and too far away, he simply gazes at it and paints it instead.

We need not stop to criticize this account, for I'm sure that every artist in history would clearly recognize this account of his aesthetic experience as "certain," just as you say. That is clearly the explanation of the iconography of haloes.

FREUD: I know this interpretation seems strange to most people. But I do not accept the authority of majority opinion, Socrates.

SOCRATES: Oh, that's very clear.

FREUD: I accept only the authority of reality. I am a realist. I look at data, at facts, not ideals.

SOCRATES: Then you must realize that almost everyone in the world, the learned as well as the unlearned, would find utterly *un*realistic your account of love—of all forms of love, including aesthetic love *and* family affection, and even your account of romantic love, which is the distinctively human version of erotic love. According to your account, if Romeo had really understood what was going on in his subconscious, what he would have said to Juliet, instead of his overly-idealistic, artificially-spiritual proposal of romance, would have been something like this: "My genital needs have led me to found a family and I have chosen you as my sexual object."

FREUD: Again you turn to satire instead of argument, Socrates.

SOCRATES: Not at all. I am merely checking with you to see whether my words are an accurate mirror of your thoughts. Do you say now that they are not?

FREUD: No, I object to your sarcastic tone, not your words themselves.

SOCRATES: Then if my words do reflect your thoughts, as you admit they do, it follows that when you call these words satire you call your thoughts self-satire.

Is that your secret? Is this whole edifice that you have erected, this whole new supposed science that you have discovered, with its central thesis of the divinity of sex, the absoluteness and ubiquitous first-cause status of genital sex—is this perhaps the world's most elaborate, colossal joke?

This changes everything. I had been suspicious of your thoughts until this point, Sigmund, but now I see that perhaps you are actually much cleverer than you appear to be. Perhaps your whole life's output has really been an astonishingly brilliant and elaborate "reductio ad absurdum." And you have hoodwinked the whole world into believing that it was not a joke or a satire at all, but serious. What an embarrassment will appear on everyone's face, and what a laugh will emerge from yours, when the world discovers the single greatest sentence you have ever written; the sentence that will transfer all your other sentences from the category of absurdity into the category of brilliance. That sentence you must have written somewhere, perhaps on a sealed document that was buried with you in your coffin and that will be exhumed and read only 100 years after your death. It is the sentence: "Everything I have ever written is a joke."

I bow my knee in awe now that I envisage that possibility, for I think I am in the presence of the greatest comedian of all time!

FREUD: I will no longer dignify your sarcasm with a serious reply. As you well know, I am quite serious in what I say, Socrates.

SOCRATES: Then I had better become serious in examining it.

FREUD: But the central problem of my book is not this reduction of *agape* to *eros* but the paradox of civilization, which you have not yet examined.

SOCRATES: So let us turn to that, then.

13.
Life's Great *Koan* Puzzle: You Can't *Ever* Get What You Want

SOCRATES: You now sum up the results of your election. Not a single candidate for the position of president of human life, greatest good, supreme value, happiness, or even the minimization of misery, has been elected. None deserves our vote. None can solve life's problem.

FREUD: And of course you will now satirize my pessimism, I suppose.

SOCRATES: On the contrary, this is where I think you become quite profound.

FREUD: "Quite profound"? I did not expect such a compliment from you, Socrates.

SOCRATES: You should. You have a brilliant and incisive mind, and you write a book that is eminently worth reading, even though I think it contains many errors which are not only ridiculous but inexcusable and disastrous.

FREUD: How can you say both of those things in the same sentence?

SOCRATES: Because it takes the most extreme brilliance to fall into the most extreme folly, and therefore when we find extreme folly we are also likely to find, in the next paragraph, extreme wisdom.

FREUD: I don't know whether I am being damned with faint praise or praised with faint damn.

SOCRATES: Neither of the two is faint, Sigmund. Both are "extreme." And both are sincere.

FREUD: Oh. Well—thank you, I think. Let's get on with the "profundity" then.

SOCRATES: You say: **In spite of the incompleteness of my enumeration, I will venture on a few remarks as a conclusion to our enquiry. The programme of becoming happy, which the pleasure principle imposes on us, cannot be fulfilled; yet we must not—indeed, we cannot—give up our efforts to bring it nearer to fulfillment by some means or other.** And here you refer to a previous passage about the "pleasure principle," where you said: **There can be no doubt about its efficacy, and yet its programme is at loggerheads with the whole world . . . there is no possibility at all of its being carried through; all the regulations of the universe run counter to it.**

What an astonishing situation! At the very heart of human life lies a *koan*: a puzzle that *must* be solved yet *cannot* be solved. If "all the regulations of the universe run counter to it," I am surprised that you do not question it. If this "it" referred to anything other than the pleasure principle, you would surely regard the fact that "all the regulations of the universe run counter to it" as a refutation of "it", and you would abandon "it." For as a materialist you believe that there is nothing in man that transcends the universe—no soul or spirit—and therefore "the regulations of the universe" are your supreme authority. Why do you not question the pleasure principle, then?

FREUD: Because the pleasure principle is as inseparable from human nature as these regulations, which cause us pain, are inseparable from the universe.

SOCRATES: I see. What a predicament! The contradiction between the "pleasure principle" and the "reality principle" is a problem as intolerable in practice as a logical self-contradiction in theory.

Why, then, do you not take this predicament as a sign that you have made some mistake in the thinking that led to it? When a traveler meets a dead end at the end of the road he has taken, he retraces his steps to find out where his error was, and corrects that error.

FREUD: Where could the error possibly be? We cannot change human nature, which demands the impossible, and we cannot change the universe, which refuses to supply our demands.

SOCRATES: Well, let's begin by backing up and looking at the larger picture. Often, that is the only way out of a problem when the close view shows absolutely no exit.

Logically, there are only two possible places to look for an error, for there are two things that collide here, two things your thinking puts at loggerheads: human nature and the nature of the universe, or subjective reality and objective reality. Is that not so?

FREUD: Yes.

SOCRATES: Well, then, either you were wrong about the regulations of the universe or you were wrong about man.

FREUD: But the universe does in fact thwart us and pain us, and man does in fact desire not to be thwarted and pained!

SOCRATES: Indeed. And those two facts are quite obvious and quite heavy, so to speak. But perhaps they are only the surface. Perhaps there are other facts that are even heavier. Perhaps we have seen only the epidermis of the universe, or the epidermis of man. Perhaps there are also deeper "regulations of the universe," other laws that determine and control and explain and cast new light on the painful and frustrating laws you have observed. Perhaps this pain and frustration is in the long run for our *good.*

FREUD: In other words, perhaps there is a benevolent Deity who providentially arranges everything, even pain, for our greater pleasure in the end.

SOCRATES: Perhaps. Or perhaps the end we are steered to by the universe, or the deity, or whatever objective reality consists in, is not pleasure at all but something else, something that is even better for us.

FREUD: That is meaningless to me. If it is not pleasure, we are not pleased by it.

SOCRATES: Perhaps it is something that we ought to be pleased by but are not. Perhaps, in other words, human nature is inherently foolish.

FREUD: What could this "something" be?

SOCRATES: Perhaps it is wisdom and virtue, as we old Greeks and Romans thought. Perhaps we *need* to experience unpleasure and pain and frustration to attain these greater goods. Perhaps we would become silly, shallow, stupid, spoiled brats if the universe obeyed our desires all the time. In fact, I would say this "perhaps" is nearly a certainty, for it is the teaching of almost all the wise men of almost every age and place and culture except yourself. Might it be that it is you, rather than the universe *and* mankind, who have made a mistake?

FREUD: But that is the religious view. Your "perhaps" amounts to saying that perhaps "all things work together for good" because there is a God, who is both all-powerful, and thus in control of every event, and also all-wise, and thus aware of exactly what each of us needs for his eventual happiness, and also all-benevolent, and thus His end and will is our own highest happiness, and therefore He uses every event in the universe, including the cooling of the earth's crust and the evolution of animal species and the coming together of a certain sperm and a certain ovum and the fall of every sparrow and hair and cancer cell—that He arranges all these things, even horrors, as means to the end of our greatest good. Ultimately, that is what is entailed in your alternative hypothesis.

SOCRATES: What an amazing scenario! I think you are more religious than I am, Sigmund. And if this is what is meant, therefore . . . what?

FREUD: Talk about a reductio ad absurdum—there's the biggest one of all! And you don't even recognize it? I was speaking in satire, Socrates. That scenario would be the perfect fairy tale, *obviously* a case of supreme wishful thinking, far too good to be true.

SOCRATES: "Too good to be true"—do you realize the assumption that that principle carries?

FREUD: What?

SOCRATES: That ultimately, reality is *not* good; that "not-good" trumps and judges and explains "good" rather than vice versa. That "real" (or "true") and "good" point in opposite directions.

FREUD: Alas, that is the case. That is "the reality principle."

SOCRATES: I see you believe that terrible pessimism. But you do not *have* to believe that. It is a faith, a choice.

FREUD: It is a necessity.

SOCRATES: Many believe the opposite.

FREUD: The fairy tale? It is impossible.

SOCRATES: Only what is self-contradictory is impossible. And this other view does not seem to be self-contradictory. Therefore it is not impossible. Therefore it is possible. Therefore it is *possible* that your choice, your ultimate pessimism, is mistaken.

FREUD: There is abundant evidence for my pessimism, and none for optimism.

SOCRATES: On the contrary, the optimist can explain all your evidence for pessimism quite logically, can explain pain as something we need for the wisdom and virtue that are necessary for the deeper good, the deeper happiness.

FREUD: And I can equally explain the optimist's optimism as wishful thinking, as I did in my two books that debunk religion.

SOCRATES: You can indeed. So we are left with a free choice. And since both options are logically possible, and only one gives you hope and happiness, why would you choose the hopeless one?

FREUD: Because there is reason and evidence for it, and none for the other one.

SOCRATES: But many thinkers have given positive reasons for believing this other one.

FREUD: But they are so easily and obviously explainable as wishful thinking!

SOCRATES: Why do you find such an explanation so easy and so obvious—more so than any of your predecessors have done?

FREUD: Because I have discovered the mechanisms of the human psyche, and I have discovered that ultimately *all* thinking is wishful thinking.

SOCRATES: Unlike *your* thinking?

FREUD: How could pessimism be wishful thinking?

SOCRATES: Oh, I think you can easily answer that question with a little common sense psychology. The desire to insult and hurt a parent or a parent figure—a God, perhaps—for allowing you pain without explaining why. Or your own Oedipus complex—surely you can explain the psychological origin of atheism very well by your own principles! You had a very bad relationship with your father, and you subconsciously wanted him dead, so you transferred that death-wish to God the Father. You see, Sigmund, two can always play at your game of psychological reductionism. The suspicions always cancel each other out and leave us with the original question.

FREUD: And if that is true, where do you say this leaves us now with regard to *our* original question, our common problem, the problem of unhappiness?

SOCRATES: It seems that credible reasons can be given for both sides—for both what we could call ultimate optimism and ultimate pessimism, for both the religious view and the atheistic view, for *both* beliefs about the final Truth about human life: that it is good and that it is not good. Theoretically, each side can explain the other's data. Neither side is definitively refuted by the data. And neither side is logically impossible, neither side is directly logically self-contradictory.

FREUD: Then as far as *our* dialog is concerned, we seem to have a standoff.

SOCRATES: *Theoretically*, we may have a standoff. But not practically. We are not only theorists and thinkers but also practitioners and actors. What about the practical consequences of each of these two choices? We have not yet considered that question.

FREUD: A large question, Socrates.

SOCRATES: But essentially a very simple one. For one option ends in your dead end, your practical self-contradiction, and the other does not. Why, then, would you deliberately prefer the dead end? Can you give me a logical reason for preferring hopelessness and pessimism and cynicism?

FREUD: Perhaps not.

SOCRATES: Then if there is no logical reason, it must be a psychological reason. So I think what you need is not a philosopher but a psychoanalyst.

But that is not my task. I will leave that to Another. Inquiry into the unique ins and outs of your individual psyche are not within my competence.

However, your philosophy is. And here is another possible source of error. When we asked about the sources of your *koan,* your "loggerheads" between man and the universe, we noted that there were two possible areas of error: the two parties to the loggerheads: the universe and man. We have considered the possibility that you were in error about "the regulations of the universe," that perhaps the material universe was only the epidermis. Now we should look at the other possibility: that you were wrong about man. Perhaps there too you see only the epidermis.

FREUD: But it was I who penetrated *below* the epidermis, the obvious, conscious level, and explored the inner jungle of the unconscious and the subconscious for the first time.

SOCRATES: How then do you explain the fact that according to Plato in book 9 of the "Republic," written 1300 years before you were born, it was I who discovered the most important principles of your psychology: the existence and power of the unconscious, the mechanisms of repression, the analysis of dreams, and even the Oedipus complex?

FREUD: You (or Plato) may have guessed these things, in a primitive form. But I did it scientifically, and I explored much farther than you or anyone else before me. Others had landed on the beach of this new continent; I explored the inland jungles.

SOCRATES: Perhaps it was you who only landed on the beach. Let's see. The next section, chapter 3, is where you explore the paradox about civilization: the paradox that the very thing we invented to make us content is the thing that makes us discontent instead. It is in the beginning of this chapter that I think you may have missed something beyond the epidermis, the obvious, in human nature. Shall we explore this now?

FREUD: Explore away, Socrates.

14.
The Paradox of Civilization: The *Cure* for Unhappiness Is the *Cause* of It

SOCRATES: Here is how you begin the central section of your book, which introduces your paradox about civilization. It is a *sociological* point, a point about civilization rather than individuals. But I would like to explore your more hidden *psychological* point first, in your first paragraph.

It reads:

Our enquiry concerning happiness has not so far taught us much that is not already common knowledge. And even if we proceed from it to the problem of why it is so hard for men to be happy, there seems to be no greater prospect of learning anything new. We have given the answer already by pointing to the three sources from which our suffering comes: the superior power of nature, the feebleness of our own bodies, and the inadequacy of the regulations which adjust the mutual relationships of human beings in the family, the state and society.

I think this is a very useful classification, especially since your next point is that we all instinctively react to the problems posed to us by this third source of suffering very differently than we react to the other two. We accept the first two but we protest against the third because we think it is our own fault. You say: **In regard to the first two sources, our judgment cannot hesitate long. It forces us to acknowledge those sources of suffering and to submit to the inevitable. We shall never completely master nature; and our bodily organism, itself a part of that nature, will always remain a transient structure** (how delicately you put the fact that we *die*!) **with a limited capacity for adaption and achievement. This recognition does not have a paralyzing effect. On the contrary, it points the direction for our activity. If we cannot remove all suffering, we can remove some, and we can mitigate some: the experience of many thousands of years has convinced us of that. As regards the third source of suffering, our attitude is a different one. We do not admit it at all; we cannot see why the regulations made by ourselves should not, on the contrary, be a protection and a benefit for every one of us.**

Can you explain why "we do not admit it at all" with regard to this third factor, which you call "civilization"?

FREUD: It is obvious. We are surprised and confused and even outraged at civilization precisely because all these things that constitute civilization—all the "auxiliary constructions," as I put it earlier, are made by ourselves for that very purpose, to fulfill the "pleasure principle" or at least to make progress in that direction. And since these "auxiliary constructions" *come from our will* rather than from the impersonal forces of nature and our own bodily fragility and mortality which *frustrate* and oppose our will, we expect these "auxiliary constructions" that I call "civilization" to help our side in this great war, this "loggerheads," to work for happiness rather rather than for the side of our enemy, unhappiness. The reason we are outraged and surprised is that it does the opposite. And that is the paradox of civilization: that the very thing we devise to relieve suffering—"civilization"—adds to our suffering!

SOCRATES: I admire your honest and innocent surprise here, Sigmund, and your fascination with the surprising, the paradoxical, and the previously unknown. It is the mark of a good hunter to focus on the darkest bushes, where the game is most likely to hide. Thus you speak here of **a contention which is so astonishing that we must dwell upon it. This contention holds that what we call our civilization is largely responsible for our misery, and that we should be much happier if we gave it up and returned to primitive conditions.**

Rousseau is probably the most famous representative of this position among the philosophers; but it is popular among the masses, as is evident from the fact that when people go on vacations, when they devise what they intend to be maximally happy circumstances for themselves, they typically go to primitive places, turning back the clock to simpler and happier times.

Do you agree with Rousseau and the masses here?

FREUD: I confess that I must be agnostic about this. I do certainly agree that mankind feels at best ambivalent about civilization and at worst betrayed by it—if that were not so, I would not have written this book or given it its title—but I do not know whether or not our ancestors were actually happier than we are, as we tend to think they were. As I say a few pages later, **It seems certain that we do not feel comfortable in our present-day civilization, but it is very difficult to form an opinion**

whether and in what degree men of an earlier age felt happier and what part their cultural conditions played in the matter.

SOCRATES: So you leave open the possibility that something other than "cultural conditions," or "civilization," may have made them happier.

FREUD: Indeed. In fact, I suggest that the causes were more psychological than cultural or anthropological or sociological. I say: **when we consider how unsuccessful we have been in precisely this field of prevention of suffering, a suspicion dawns on us that here, too, a piece of unconquerable nature may lie behind—this time a piece of our own psychical constitution.**

That is a fourth and deeper and more hidden source of suffering, and the rest of my book explores it. It is all about the mechanisms of repression that are simultaneously necessary for civilization and frustrating to the pleasure principle.

SOCRATES: Whether you have defined its causality correctly or not, you certainly seem to have defined its location. If it is not outside us, or in our own bodies, then it must be in our own psyches.

FREUD: And what else could it be if not the mechanisms of repression?

SOCRATES: I don't know until I look. But shouldn't we look more deeply at the symptoms before we rush into the details of your diagnosis of their cause? In fact, that is the very thing you do in your book, when you explain people's discontent with the advances of modern civilization. And I must say that what you say here seems very reasonable to me:

During the last few generations mankind has made an extraordinary advance in the natural sciences and in their technical application and has established his control over nature in a way never before imagined.

This is certainly true. I think if a medieval peasant had been brought by a time machine into one of our modern cities, he would probably believe that God had sent that city supernaturally down from Heaven rather than man building it up naturally from earth. Would a medieval Mongolian think the Empire State Building was really only a large yurt? If he saw a computer, would he not think a spirit was inside it?

The single steps of this advance are common knowledge and it is unnecessary to enumerate them. Men are proud of those achievements, and have a right to be. But they seem to have observed that this newly-won power over space and time, this subjugation of the forces of nature, which is the fulfillment of a longing that goes back thousands of years, has not increased the amount of pleasurable satisfaction which they may expect from life and has not made them feel happier. . . .

A little later, you make the same point even more poignantly: **These things that, by his science and technology, man has brought about on this earth, on which he first appeared as a feeble animal organism and on which each individual of his species must once more make its entry ("oh inch of nature!") as a helpless suckling—these things do not only sound like a fairy tale, they are an actual fulfillment of every—or of almost every—fairy tale wish. All these assets he may lay claim to as his cultural acquisition. Long ago he formed an ideal conception of omnipotence and omniscience which he embodied in his gods. To these gods he attributed everything that seemed unattainable to his wishes,**

or that was forbidden to him. One may say, therefore, that these gods were cultural ideals. Today he has come very close to the attainment of this ideal, he has almost become a god himself. . . .

Future ages will bring with them new and probably unimaginably great advances in the field of civilization and will increase man's likeness to God still more But in the interests of our investigations, we will not forget that present-day man does not feel happy in his Godlike character.

I admire your honesty, Sigmund, in confessing this puzzle and your puzzlement at it. It would have been easy for you to have done what so many other atheists have done, namely to ignore this question and to extol these secular scientific achievements as proof of the superiority of atheism over religion. For religion did not encourage the scientific and technological "conquest of nature" as much as atheism did, since atheism claimed that the most important thing in life was not to conform man's will to God but nature to man's will. This new answer to the great question of the "greatest good" or the "meaning of life"—science and technology—has been spectacularly successful, perhaps even more successful than religion ever was. For man has had far more success in making nature conform to himself than in making himself conform to God. Yet this has *not* been successful in making us happy.

You dare to look at these facts and honestly admit, even though you are an atheist, that the secular program has been a failure. It has not attained its end. For the end is not science and technology. They are only means. The end is happiness. We have exchanged our gods for machines, but our machines have not made us any happier than our gods did.

So now you dare to honestly confront the overwhelmingly obvious question that so many other defenders of the new order have not dared to confront, namely: *Why are we not happy?* And even more wonderful than that, you dare to honestly confess that you do not know the answer to that question!

You dare to do this even though it is an admission of data that bring your atheism into question.

FREUD: How does it bring atheism into question?

SOCRATES: As any scientific theory is brought into question by empirical data that run counter to what the theory predicts.

For let us suppose that the theory of atheism is true, and all gods are mere wishful thinking. Why did we indulge in such fantasy? Because we seek happiness, of course. We invented these beings who conquer space, time and matter because we could not do those things when science and technology were still primitive. But we *could* invent gods who could do these things, and thus we could enjoy these divine powers vicariously, and this became a kind of collective dream called religion. This is part of your theory of the origin of religion—it originates in fantasizing and wishful thinking, which is the obverse of fear.

If this theory is true, then the more godlike we become, the more happy we will be. But we observe the opposite result from the one predicted by the theory: we have realized our dreams, we have become more and more godlike but *not* more and more happy. In fact we have become more and more *un*happy.

Why?

Your first answer is to confess that you do not know. I find this admirable—a kind of humility and honesty—the two virtues for which I am (undeservedly) famous.

FREUD: I suppose you will now suggest that perhaps the reason modern man is not happier than ancient man even though he is more Godlike in power and knowledge is that he is not more Godlike in holiness or saintliness, or something like that. You will say that the data show that religion makes men happier than technology does, and you will then explain *why* this is so by quoting the famous line of Saint Augustine: "Thou hast made us for Thyself, and therefore our hearts are restless until they rest in Thee."

SOCRATES: That is one possible explanation, though I do not claim to know it is the correct one. I am an agnostic, not an apologist. Do you have another explanation?

FREUD: In addition to what I say later about the mechanisms of repression, I hint at another answer here when I say that **Man has, as it were, become a kind of prosthetic God. When he puts on all his auxiliary organs he is truly magnificent; but those organs have not grown on to him and they still give him much trouble at times.**

SOCRATES: I see. Technology is like a set of powerful prosthetic limbs, but they do not make the human muscles that operate them any more powerful. If anything, they make them weaker.

FREUD: And the problem is exacerbated by the fact that the man inside the prosthesis becomes *addicted* to it, and to its power, as a magician might be addicted to a magic ring.

SOCRATES: Or as a drug addict or alcoholic would be addicted to his pain-relieving chemical—which you called the "most efficient" answer to life's greatest problem!

FREUD: I do not defend addiction, and I warn against it. You do not refute my suggestion that way, Socrates.

SOCRATES: I did not think that I did. In fact, I find your suggestion quite profound, and very similar to what you said about the deepest source of unhappiness being something in human nature itself. That sounds quite similar to the religious explanation. The religious might call this innate addiction to power "Original Sin," or "Original Selfishness."

So the hypothesis you open yourself to considering here is that perhaps, as the religious say, we are made happy not by what we *have* but by what we *are*. And perhaps also, as they say, we are made happy by being *good*, by wisdom and virtue, by unselfishness, by loving, more than by anything else, and by *agape* more than by *eros*. The data, at least, seem to support that hypothesis.

FREUD: There are always many hypotheses that can be invented to explain a set of data. No one of them can ever be proved with mathematical certainty, because scientific proof is inductive and incremental and gradual and probable, while mathematical proof is deductive and conclusive and final. That is why I end on a note of agnosticism—which I had thought you would admire for its humility and honesty.

15.
The Conclusion: Freud's Only Certainty: Absolute Relativism

SOCRATES: Do you indeed end on that note? Let us see. Let us examine your last two paragraphs.

FREUD: Why do you omit exploring many pages of the second half of my book in which I explore the way civilization inevitably represses our sexual instincts?

SOCRATES: Because it is highly speculative theorizing, which depends on the truth of many details of your psychoanalytical system, which you use as premises or presuppositions. These are not proved. I am thinking especially your assumption of sexual reductionism, reducing everything apparently nonsexual to something sexual. I do not know how to argue about such a theory. It does not seem to me to be a truly scientific theory at all.

FREUD: Why not? It is based on empirical data—case histories—and it is used to explain the data, theoretically, and it leads to cures, practically. It works. So why do you think it is not truly scientific?

SOCRATES: Because it is not falsifiable. Whatever data you run into in your therapy, you will simply interpret in terms of your principles: your reductionistic pan-sexualism, your materialism, your pleasure principle, and your id-ego-superego dynamics. But a theory is not scientific if it is not falsifiable, if it is so "stretchable" that it can cover any and all possible data. That is like the faith that God is good, and trustable, no matter how many apparently pointless evils He allows His beloved children to experience, as He did to Job. It is a religious belief, not a scientific theory.

You will also have to interpret all criticisms of your theory in terms of that theory: as motivated by sexual repression, or id-superego conflict. That is the kind of argument that leads nowhere, as I said before. It is a double "ad hominem." Both parties can use it, and then we are back where we were before, looking at the objective data and rational arguments instead of at each other. That is why I want to pass over all these technical and questionable psychological details in the second half of your book and look at your conclusion.

FREUD: I'm kind of proud of "all these technical and questionable psychological details," Socrates. But I'd also like to end this purgatory with you, so I'm happy to skip it with you. Let's look at my conclusion, then.

SOCRATES: You write there:

For a wide variety of reasons, it is very far from my intention to express an opinion upon the value of human civilization. I have endeavored to guard myself against the enthusiastic prejudice which holds that our civilization is the most precious thing that we possess or could acquire and that its path will necessarily lead to heights of unimagined perfection. I can at least listen without indignation to the critic who is of the opinion that when one surveys the aims of cultural endeavour

and the means it employs, one is bound to come to the conclusion that the whole effort is not worth the trouble, and that the outcome of it can only be a state of affairs which the individual will be unable to tolerate.

So you neither affirm nor deny this Rousseauian position.

FREUD: Yes. I am agnostic: a good position for a scientist and a philosopher, I think. It keeps one impartial.

SOCRATES: But you next say that **My impartiality is made all the easier to me by my knowing very little about all these things.** Surely that is a mistake: impartiality does not stem from ignorance but from knowledge. Is a stupid judge more impartial than a wise one?

FREUD: That was a slip of the pen.

SOCRATES: But the next thing you say is, to my mind, the very worst and most impossible thing you have ever said, and the one sentence in your book which is absolutely and self-evidently false. Yet you claim it as the one thing you are certain of, and *not* agnostic about! You say:

One thing only do I know for certain and that is that man's judgments of value follow directly his wishes for happiness—that, accordingly, they are an attempt to support his illusions with arguments.

Do you see why I find this logically self-contradictory?

FREUD: I don't want to guess, Socrates. Just tell me your argument.

SOCRATES: It is the logical argument against all forms of skepticism: that they are all self-contradictory, because the skeptic says he knows that he does not know, or is certain that no one is ever certain, or that it is true that there is no truth, or that it is an absolute that there are no absolutes, or that it is universally true that there are no universal truths, or that it is an objective truth that truth is not objective.

FREUD: And which of these self-contradictions do you say I am guilty of?

SOCRATES: A form of the last one. You say that "man's judgments of value . . . are an attempt to support his illusions with arguments." So you claim that all reasoning about values is rationalizing, the rationalizing of personal desire. We all believe what we believe not because of an honest receptivity of the mind to truth but only because we *desire* to believe it because we think it will make us happy. In other words, your "pleasure principle" rules not only the emotions and the will but also the mind with an absolute tyranny. In which case no one's opinion about values is to be trusted—including yours, in this book!

You may as well have told us that from the beginning, warning us on page one that this book only *pretends* to say something universally and objectively true but really only expresses its author's individual and subjective desires for happiness. But in that case no one would read it, unless he wanted to psychoanalyze you.

Of all the things to claim certainty about, this is the worst one you could possibly have chosen. Any of the other sentences in your book—there are over a thousand of them—*might* be true, but this one *could* not be true, because it immediately and directly contradicts itself. It destroys its own authority. It is a confession of absolute relativism.

FREUD: What is *your* absolute, Socrates? If I were to ask you to rewrite my sentence, how would you end it? What is the one thing *you* claim to know for certain?

SOCRATES: That everything—everything that is and everything that happens, every entity and every quality and every event—has a reason. A reason why it exists and a reason why it is what it is. And that sometimes we can know that reason. That *not* all reasoning is rationalizing. In other words, the exact opposite of yours. And I think my absolute is the foundation of science and yours is the foundation of superstition.

FREUD: I suppose we will just have to agree to disagree about that, then, Socrates. I think our conversation is over. We have at least made this bit of progress, I think: we have finally unearthed our deepest disagreement, and the reason for all our other disagreements.

SOCRATES: I agree with your conclusion, Sigmund: we can go no further.

16.
What Next?

FREUD: Where do I go now, then? You are apparently acquainted with this place better than I am, whether this place is real, or whether it is my dream.

SOCRATES: You have only been analyzed. You now will be psychoanalyzed.

FREUD: Hoist by my own petard, eh? Who will be my therapist?

SOCRATES: A psychologist named Paul Vitz. He has written a book about you using your own techniques to explain your life and your opinions. You could hardly ask for anything fairer than that.

FREUD: And after that?

SOCRATES: I cannot say.

FREUD: Where do *you* go next, Socrates?

SOCRATES: To another dialog like this one, to explore another philosopher's little book.

FREUD: Which philosopher, if I may ask?

SOCRATES: Søren Kierkegaard, a Danish existentialist.

FREUD: What is an "existentialist"?

SOCRATES: An explorer of human existence, individually, concretely, personally, and subjectively.

FREUD: He sounds like a psychoanalyst.

SOCRATES: Far from it.

FREUD: I never heard of him.

SOCRATES: You wouldn't have. He remained obscure for almost a hundred years, until shortly after your death some Americans translated him into English, and he suddenly became world famous.

FREUD: Did *he* have any one claim to certainty, as both of us did?

SOCRATES: Actually, he did. He once wrote that even if every sentence he had ever written was false—and he wrote many books in many styles from many points of view, including many pseudonyms—the one thing that was certainly true is *that God is love.*

FREUD: He chose *that* as his one *certainty?*

SOCRATES: Yes. Strange, isn't it?

FREUD: So strange that I would say there is hardly any sentence ever uttered which seems *less* certain.

SOCRATES: So it seems. He is as far from you as I am, though in a different direction. We are like three points on a triangle. He actually is what you accused me of being: a fervent religious believer and a very clever and tricky apologist for his religion.

FREUD: Which religion?

SOCRATES: Christianity.

FREUD: So he believes that "God is love" because he believes that Jesus is literally God who became man and suffered and died out of love of mankind.

SOCRATES: Yes. The doctrine is called the "Incarnation." This man Jesus is called "the Word of God"—though I do not know what that means.

FREUD: And does he think he can prove this unbelievable teaching?

SOCRATES: Not at all. In fact he calls it "the absolute paradox." He is almost an irrationalist, but not quite, and of a very different sort than you.

FREUD: How is he different from me?

SOCRATES: In a word, according to him Jesus is "the Word became flesh." Your book, by contrast, is the flesh become word.